THE HENTY CENTURY - FERRING

Introduction

In the long history of Ferring, the years 1801 to 1900 can well be dubbed 'The Henty Century', given the dominance of the three generations of this family that leased, and finally owned outright, the principal estate in the parish, and acquired so much of the farmland and cottages as the Century went on. This continuity is reflected in the economic geography of Ferring. An aerial view in 1900 would have looked very much the same as a view of Ferring in 1801. The early maps do not show much detail but the roads and the clusters of houses around the church and the various farms hardly changed in a hundred years. The most obvious change was the disappearance of the windmill on Highdown and the appearance of the railway running through the middle of the parish.

Ferring was always a farming village – from Saxon times right up to the mid-1920s – and any aerial view would have been dominated by fields of pasture, meadow and crops. But important changes took place in the 19th Century, particularly in land ownership and management. As ever, sheep grazed on Highdown, cereals were grown on the flat land, and dairy cattle were in the meadows along the Rife and on the far side of Highdown. But the 19th Century saw the last of the arable strips in the 'common fields' (and the use of oxen to plough them) and of grazing and haymaking in the 'common meadows'. Land ownership was more and more concentrated in the hands of a few large proprietors and tenant farmers, and in the last quarter of the Century, market gardening, fruit production and horticulture had displaced some of the arable farming.

Ferring's population remained at around 50 families all through the period – 238 residents in the 1801 census and 243 in the 1901 census - dictated by the limited availability of work and the 'tied cottages' provided by the farmers. But the make-up of that population did change a little over this period: from the long lists of agricultural labourers and servants of the 1841 census to the wider social span of the 1881, 1891 and 1901 returns. There were more independent tradesmen, and new occupations such as elementary school teacher, postman, railwayman, and shopkeeper. There were also more 'gentry' – not just the principal land owner and the Vicar but a retired doctor, a retired army officer, substantial farmers and some people of 'independent means'.

Public administration also changed, but again, only towards the end of the Century. There had been two manors in Ferring – the Bishop of Chichester's manor of Ferring and Fure (West Ferring and a detached area near Billingshurst) and the much smaller manor of East Ferring (which had separated from the Bishop's manor in the middle ages), where the Westbrook/Richardson family had been Lords of the Manor since the middle of the 17th Century. The main manor court continued to make decisions on tenancies, fences, ditches, stray animals and so on all through the Century although in the 1860s the Lordship was transferred to the Ecclesiastical Commissioners. The East Ferring manor was still holding its court in 1779 but there were only a handful of tenants, and these were being pursued for non-attendance, and by 1801 any necessary business was probably conducted in the Manor Court of Goring.

The Parish and its Vestry meetings still had certain civil responsibilities for most of the Century. Its responsibility for the Poor Law had been syndicated with four neighbouring parishes in 1790 in a Union Workhouse at East Preston, but the Parish still had to collect the Poor Rate. Its responsibility for local roads was only taken over by the District Council in 1894. The ecclesiastical role of the parish involved much more than the organisation and maintenance of St Andrew's Church. It provided alms (including an annual Church Dole up to the 1860s) and was very much involved with the provision of education – initially with Sunday Schools, taught by the clergy, and later, in conjunction with the National Society for the Education of the Poor in the Principles of the Established Church, setting up a 'National' elementary school in 1873.

In 1875 Public Health legislation set up Sanitary Authorities all across England, to ensure fresh water, adequate sewerage, refuse disposal and safe food. These authorities had elected members and Ferring was represented on the East Preston Sanitary Authority, which covered the same area as the Workhouse Union. The 1888 Local Government Act set up the County Councils, taking over from the Quarter Sessions responsibility for the main roads and certain regulatory functions (Sussex was divided into East and West). Finally the 1894 Act set up the District Councils, taking over from the Sanitary Authorities, and adding responsibility for maintaining local roads. The Act also established Annual Parish Meetings of all electors, with an option to form a Parish Council. Ferring did not opt for this until 1919.

Another important change was the building of the railway from Shoreham to Chichester in 1846, with a station at Goring less than a mile away. This made it possible to travel to Brighton in less than an hour and to London in less than two hours and displaced the coaching services on which travellers had relied in the first half of the century. It also made it possible to send, later in the century, flowers, fruit and vegetables from the smallholdings to the London markets.

This period of Ferring's history is well documented. The key sources are the Census returns for 1801 to 1901, the Parish Registers, the Land Tax records (from 1801-1832), the Tithe Commutation map of 1837 and the schedules to the Agreement of 1840 (which converted tenths of produce in kind into monetary payments), the Manor Court records (for West Ferring), the Ordnance Survey maps (1813, 1876 and 1899), Kelly's street directories, the Times and local newspapers. There are, of course, few photographs to illustrate this account.

As in 'The Day before Yesterday', the material is presented by theme as well as by chronology. The first seven chapters examine land ownership, the village economy, poverty and crime, the social institutions, social life, buildings and families; the last chapter looks at the Century decade by decade. This entails a certain amount of repetition but the two methods give context to events and developments during this long span of years.

The author would like to acknowledge his debt to Ron Kerridge and Michael Standing, for their 'Ferring Past' [Philimore, 1990] and to Dr Chris Lewis for his 'Victoria County History, Sussex, Vol V.2' [Institute of Historical Research, 2009], both excellent sources. Thanks are also due to the County Archivist and Search Room staff at West Sussex Record Office.

Contents

Chapter 1: Land ownership	5
Chapter 2: The Village Economy	11
Chapter 3: Poverty, Crime and the Workhouse	17
Chapter 4: The Church, Education and Public Services	21
Chapter 5: Social Life	27
Chapter 6: Buildings	31
Chapter 7: Families	37
Chapter 8: Chronicle – a journal of life in Ferring	45
1801 – 1810	45
1811 – 1820	47
The Eighteen-Twenties	51
The Eighteen-Thirties	53
The Eighteen – Forties	55
The Eighteen-Fifties	57
The Eighteen – Sixties	59
The Eighteen – Seventies	61
The Eighteen – Eighties	63
The Eighteen – Nineties	64

Ferring in 1795

Gardner and Gream 1795. The long dashed line W to SE may indicate the boundary of Poling Hundred, an ancient jurisdiction which Ferring had left some centuries earlier.

CHAPTER 1: LAND OWNERSHIP

For many centuries, Ferring's landholdings had been dominated by the Bishop of Chichester - because of the size of his estate (leased out by 1535 but still with substantial 'service' obligations as well as money payments) and because he was Lord of the Manor for almost the whole parish. His Steward controlled the rest of the manor (under tenancies) through the Manor Court. The Bishop's estate had been leased to the Henty family since 1786. The Hentys held the lease all through the 19th Century, at times farming the land themselves, at others letting parts or all of it to tenant farmers.

The holdings of the Bishop's own tenants were recorded in the Manor Court Book, and a copy of the entry was given to the tenant. Most of these 'copyhold' tenancies were hereditary (on payment of a renewal fee) and related to a substantial area (five acres or more) of enclosed land, usually together with a house or cottage, constituting a small farm or smallholding. Some other pieces of land had been denoted in earlier centuries as 'commons', where much more modest subsistence agriculture was carried out by villagers with less capital. These villagers were allocated one-acre strips (typically 22 yards x 220 yards) in those arable fields, or the right to graze cattle in the common meadows.

Last days of strip farming
Some of these common fields still survived in the 1800s. What had been annotated as 'Ferring Towne Feilde' on the 1621 Manor survey map was now 'Ferring Common Field' and an 1804 'terrier' (plan) reproduced at the end of this chapter, shows it divided into east-west and north-south strips with a number of different occupiers. Some adjacent strips had been consolidated into a holding of three or more acres but the relics of mediaeval strip farming are clearly visible in the 1804 plan.

In earlier centuries there would have been many different owners: the plan shows only five: George Oliver Penfold, George Henty, Daniel Simmons, Thomas Martin, and the Vicar (his glebe land). George Oliver Penfold was the son of James Penfold (Vicar of Ferring 1766 – 1812). As well as owning these acres, George was heir to his father's 'Square House' (later St Maurs) and several plots in the village centre; Daniel Simmons had land elsewhere in Ferring; Thomas Martin owned five cottages in the village as well as his 18 acres in the Common Field. Henty had the lease of the manor estate. None of these were poor men struggling with subsistence farming. And Simmons did not even live in Ferring at this time.

In 1832 George Henty's son Edwin inherited the Penfold acres (his mother was Anne Penfold before her marriage), and by 1837 various amalgamations and exchanges had reduced most of the Common Field (still so called) to two owners of compact blocks– the Vicar's glebe land, (16 acres) in the northern semi-circle, and additions to Henty's farmland (40 acres) in the southern rectangle. Between the two blocks, Simmons had one 3-acre field. William Marshall (Henty's tenant in what was to be 'Home Farm') had bought the Square House in 1837, and with it 4 acres – 'Square House Field' (under grass in 1840, unlike most of the old Common Field, which was arable).

The 1837 Tithe Apportionment Map shows two other, smaller, Common Fields and a Common Meadow undergoing the same process, with many strips still delineated but amalgamated into the holdings of a few proprietors. This process of enclosure seems to have been achieved in

5

Ferring by agreement, exchange and buying-out of commoners' rights, not by legislation; and without protest (often not the case in other areas).

The 1840 Apportionment

The commutation of tithes into money payments between 1836 and 1840 required a detailed survey of land ownership and land use. The Tithe Map and the Schedules to the 1840 Agreement give a very clear account of who owned, leased or rented, what land in Ferring. The diagrams below, drawn by Richard Standing, and reproduced with his kind permission, show the distribution of ownership at that time. They also show the state of cultivation of each field – 'g' for grass, 'w' for woodland and 'f' for furze (far side of Highdown), otherwise arable.

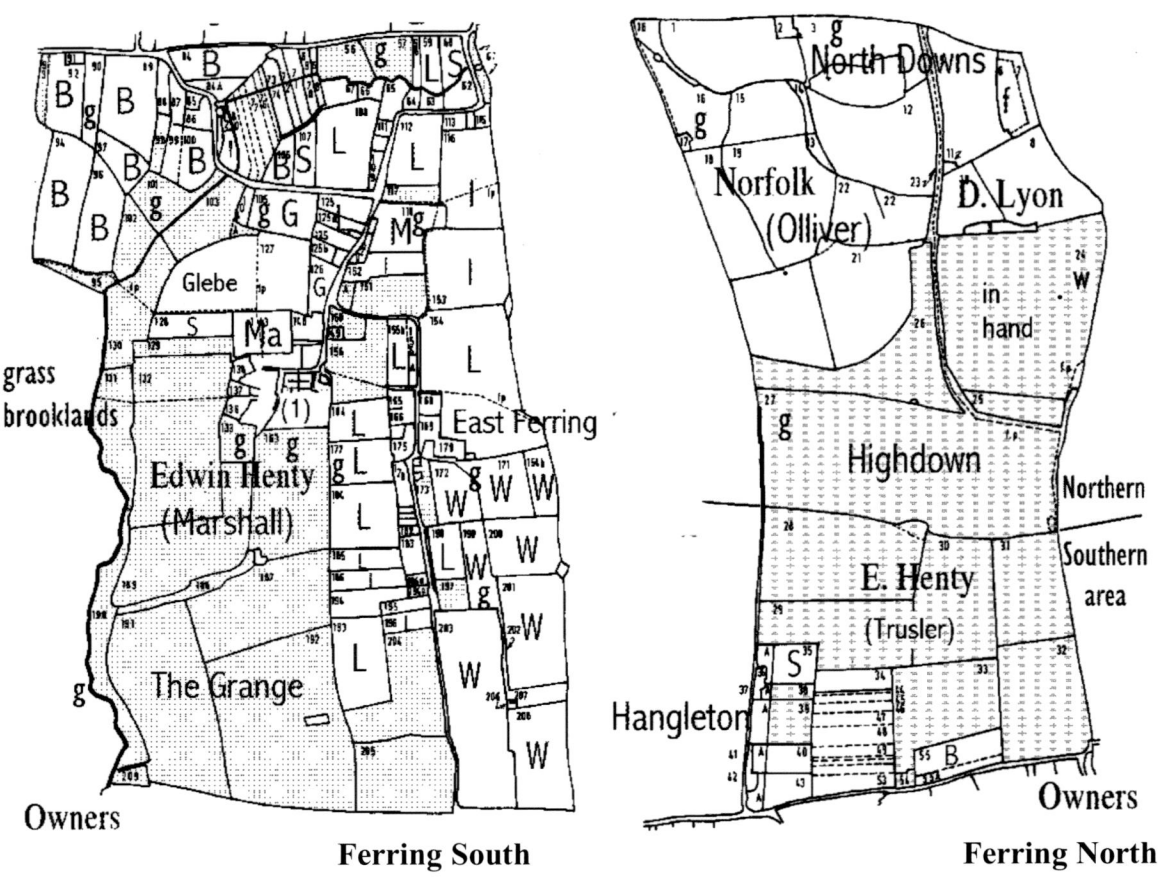

Ferring South   **Ferring North**

The holdings shown are those of Edwin Henty (and his two main tenants), David Lyon (marked 'L'), the Duke of Norfolk (and his tenant), John Bennett (marked 'B'), William Westbrook Richardson (marked 'W'), Mrs Simmons (marked 'S'), William Marshall (marked 'Ma'), Hugh Ingram (marked I) and William Monk (marked 'M').

Edwin Henty 1804-1890

The biggest holding was that of **Edwin Henty**. He had carried forward his father's and grandfather's lease of the Bishop's estate, had inherited the Penfold land from his mother, and had bought up a number of copyholds by this time, so that he now effectively owned over 450 acres (half the farmland in the parish).

From 1836 he leased most of this to tenant farmers, keeping in hand only The Coppice, north east of Highdown (probably for shooting) and the grounds of his mansion but from time to time he kept more substantial areas 'in hand' managed by a bailiff. So in the 1881 Census he is listed as 'Farmer, 176 acres, 13 employees', although his main occupation was Banker as it was in the previous Censuses.

Next came **David Lyon**, with some 200 acres, mainly in East Ferring. Lyon was a London merchant (and briefly a Member of Parliament) who had owned sugar plantations in the West Indies. As well as the income from this source he had also been given a huge sum as compensation for his losses when slavery was abolished in the British Empire in 1834. The next year he purchased the Manor of Northbrook, in Goring, from William Westbrook Richardson. He then bought 25 acres of former Richardson land in north-east Ferring in 1836, and most of East Ferring (from the Cortis family) in 1838. He had Goring Hall built for himself in 1840, a little later adding the carriage drive (now the Ilex Avenue bridle path) across to Ferring. In 1872 his Ferring estate was inherited by his brother, William, who lived at the Hall until his death in 1892, and then by his nephew William Francis Lyon.

David Lyon in 1825 by Thomas Lawrence

The **Richardson** family had inherited the Goring and East Ferring property (and much other property) from Elizabeth Richardson, granddaughter of William Westbrook (died 1702). Elizabeth named her eldest son and heir 'William Westbrook Richardson' (he died 1771). His nephew was also given the Richardson name (probably with an eye to the inheritance) and in 1828, after the death of William's son and daughter-in-law, **William Westbrook Richardson jnr** (1788- 1871) came into the considerable property (in Goring, Findon and Heene, as well as Ferring - the 69 acres, and the Farm House, at Manor Farm).

John Cortis (1757-1838) had inherited East Ferring Farm, with the farmhouse and 120 acres to the north and north-west. He had no children and left instructions in his Will that his estate should be sold, and his nephew, another John Cortis (1793-1866), to be given the first opportunity to buy it. The nephew decided not to do so but continued as the tenant on the farm when David Lyon bought it. Cortis was still the tenant in 1861 but at some point he handed over to his son, William Cortis, who by 1881 was farming 250 acres. William still gave his occupation as 'Farmer (Employer)' in the 1901 Census, although he must have retired by then. He died in 1904.

In 1840 **The Duke of Norfolk** owned 110 acres running down the north-west slope of Highdown, based on North Down Farm. Unusually for this date it was a freehold estate, previously owned by the Shelley family. It had presumably been part of the Michelgrove estate, stretching south from Patching, which the Shelley family had had since at least 1540. His tenant farmer was John Duke Olliver.

Bernard, 12th Duke of Norfolk by Henry Pickersgill

John Bennett had 56 acres, based on Hangleton farmhouse in Langbury Lane. This included strips in the Common Meadow along the upper Rife for his cattle and in Southover Common Field, just south of the farmhouse. His family had been in Ferring since at least 1559, when a marriage was recorded in the Parish Register.

Hugh Ingram had about 30 acres, somewhat scattered but mainly around the present Elm Park. **Barbara Simmons** (the Tithe apportionment refers to her as Susanna Simmons), the widow of Daniel Simmons, owned some 20 acres, including several pieces of land off Hangleton Lane (and the farmhouse at the top of the lane) and her three acres in Ferring Common Field. **William Monk** had just under 6 acres, willed to him for his lifetime by George Olliver Penfold, where the Henty Arms, the level crossing, and the Village Hall now stand.

Consolidation

All through the century, the Hentys were acquiring land, partly through marriage (George Henty's marriage to Anne Penfold) and partly by buying copyholds from tenants who were in difficulties or whose main estates were elsewhere (as when Edwin Henty bought Ingram's 30 acres in 1845). They were eventually able to 'enfranchise' these properties (convert them to freeholds) thanks to the land law reforms of the mid-century, and to the declining importance of the Manor Court. David Lyon was also extending and consolidating his holdings and in 1877 Edwin Henty and William Lyon made a series of land exchanges, involving some 60 acres each way, to make their estates more compact.

There had already been some reorganisation of Henty's farms before that, as we have seen. Edwin Henty had inherited the lease of the Bishop's estate from his father in 1829 and many properties from his mother in 1832, including half the strips in the main Common Field (few of them contiguous) and a substantial house just to the west of Ferring Grange. By exchanges with the Vicar who held various other isolated strips, he consolidated these into a 26 acre block and added them to the southern portion of the Bishop's estate to make his 'Lower Farm' (later 'Home Farm'). He advertised the tenancy of this farm of 225 acres, in July 1836. The substantial house became the farm house (later known as Home Farm House), occupied by his tenant farmers, beginning with William Marshall.

The 1836 advertisement also offered his northern farm of 180 acres to let. In the 1840 Tithe Rent Charge Apportionment, these northern acres (including Highdown) are being farmed by another tenant, Thomas Trussler, apparently based on the house we now call Franklands Manor. William Marshall (still the tenant of Home Farm), married in 1837 and in that year purchased, and moved into, 'The Square House'.

Edwin Henty continued to buy up copyholds and bought back the Square House (by 1846 known as St Maurs, and since the 1930s as Greystoke Manor), so that by his death in 1890 he owned over 600 acres (two thirds of the farmland) and numerous houses and cottages in the village. His son Edwin continued the Henty supremacy to the end of the Century.

The end of strip farming

As discussed above, the mediaeval strip farming on the Common Field survived into the early years of the 19th Century. It can be seen in the terrier (plan) of 1804 (left, with colours showing the different owners). The image has been rotated here to show the comparison with the land holdings in the Tithe Apportionment of 1840 (right).

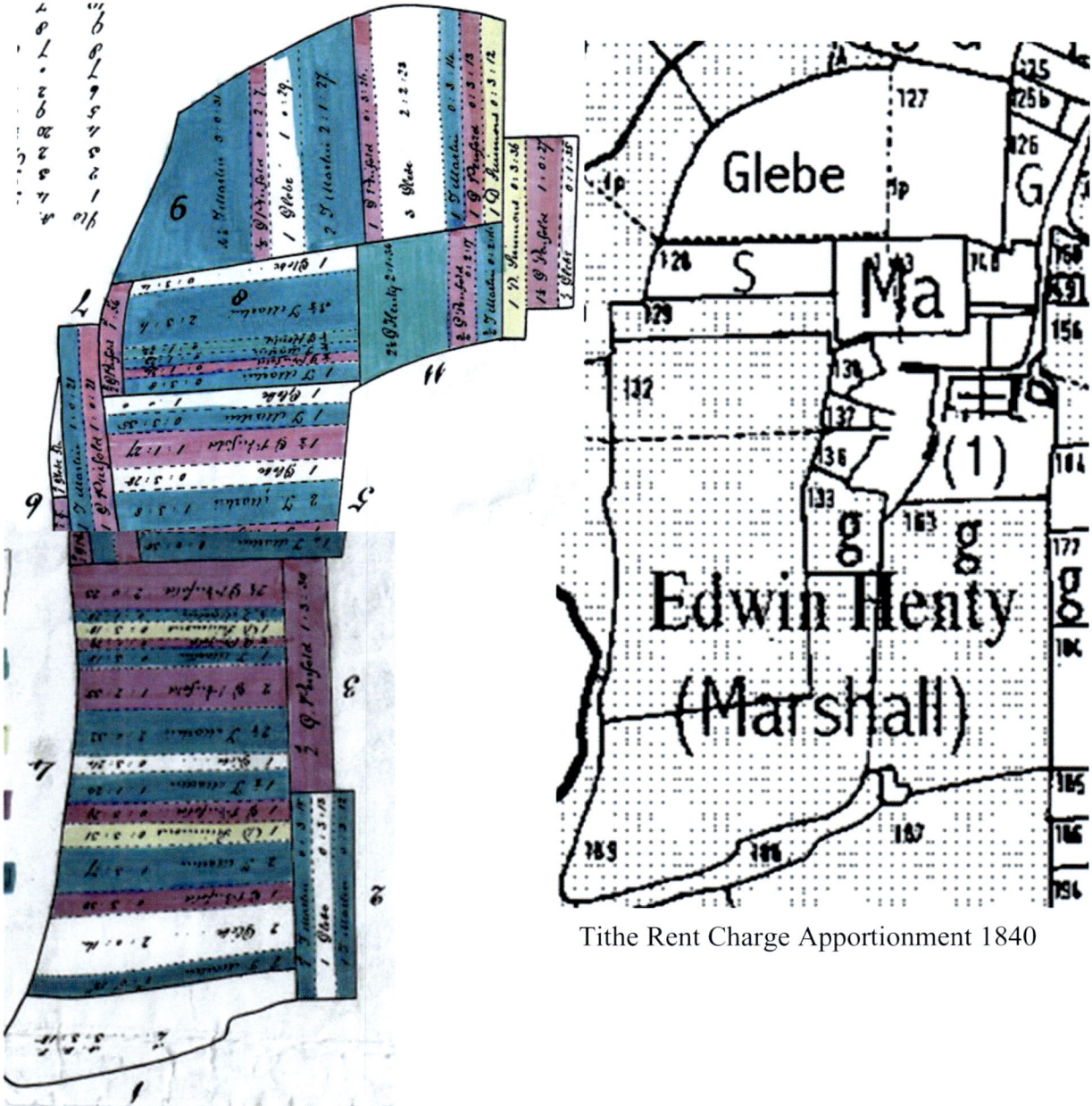

Ferring Common Field 1804

Tithe Rent Charge Apportionment 1840

WOODLANDS FARM, FERRING,

Near Patching Pond, about Two Miles from Angmering or Goring Stations, Four Miles from Arundel, and Six from Worthing.

CATALOGUE
OF THE WHOLE OF THE

LIVE AND DEAD FARMING STOCK,

COMPRISING

16 PEDIGREE SHORTHORN COWS,
BULLS, AND CALVES,
18 SOUTHDOWN TEGS,

5 large, strong, active SHIRE HORSES,
TWO 2-YEAR-OLD AND ONE YEARLING COLTS,
NAG MARE, 15 HANDS,
SUSSEX SOW, PRIZE GAME FOWLS;

Together with the capital assortment of

AGRICULTURAL IMPLEMENTS;
AND

70 OAK & OTHER TIMBER TREES,
WHICH

SPARKS AND SON

Are instructed by W. F. H. Lyon, Esq., to Sell by Auction, as above,

On Tuesday, 28th March, 1893,
AT 12.30, WITHOUT RESERVE.

Luncheon, by Ticket, 1s. 6d. each, to be returned to all purchasers, will be provided on the ground at Twelve o'Clock.

Printed at the Steam Printing Works of the *West Sussex Gazette*, Arundel.

William Lyon puts up for auction the small mixed farm on Ferring's north-eastern boundary, shortly after inheriting the Lyon estate in Goring and East Ferring.

CHAPTER 2: THE VILLAGE ECONOMY

The Farms

The Henty family increased their holdings all through the Century but were only intermittently farming the land themselves. In 1836 Edwin Henty said he was 'quitting' farming and advertised to let out his two farms (one of 180 acres in north Ferring, apparently based on 'Franklands Manor', and the 'Lower Farm' south of the village centre, 225 acres) to tenants. In the 1840 Tithe Report we see that Thomas Trussler had taken on most of the northern 180 acres and William Marshall most of the southern farm of 225 acres. In 1845 Henty acquired Franklins Green Farm (28 acres), which was also let out to a tenant, Thomas Meetens.

Trussler died in 1859 and it appears that the Cortis family took over the tenancy of the northern farm: William Cortis was certainly there in 1874. William Marshall left Ferring in 1844, and the next tenant of the southern farm was John Golds. In the 1851 Census, his occupation was listed as 'Farmer of 450 acres'. Some of it must have been outside Ferring, but it included the 225 acres of 'Lower Farm'. His other holding was probably in Goring because in 1852 he took up residence, with his large family, in the newly built Highdown Tower, as the principal tenant of David Lyon.

In that year Edwin Henty leased the Lower Farm and farmhouse to Samuel Saunders. In 1855 Saunders exhibited prize lambs at Horsham Fair but his tenure was short: he died in 1857. By 1861 Edwin Henty was employing a Bailiff to manage his land, and it was probably back 'in hand' (except for a brief period in the early 1880s), until 1908. By 1890 it was known as 'Home Farm', possibly renamed by his son, Edwin Henty jnr, when he inherited it that year. The northern farm was tenanted by the Penfold brothers from 1863 and remained so until at least 1930.

East Ferring

The Cortis family were farming their own land in East Ferring (120 acres), and living in East Ferring House, Sea Lane, until John Cortis died in 1838. The estate was then bought by David Lyon but John Cortis' nephew (another John Cortis) occupied the land and the house as a tenant until his death in 1866 The tenancy of the farm was taken on by the nephew's son, William Cortis, through to his death in 1904. Their farm was based on East Ferring Farmhouse, on Sea Lane just north of the Ilex Avenue, and that is where William Cortis lived. The Lyon family leased out East Ferring House to other occupiers for the rest of the Century.

John Cortis 1799-1866

Immediately south of the Ilex Avenue was East Ferring Manor Farm, owned by the Richardson family but let out to William Oliver. This was based on the old Manor House on the east side of Sea Lane (demolished in the early 1960s, although some ruins of the old farm buildings remain),

Hangleton

The Bennetts had been farming in Ferring since at least 1635, mainly around Langbury Lane (where their homestead still stands). In the Tithe settlement of 1840 this farm of 56 acres was shown as let out to William Knowles.

The Bennetts still owned Hangleton farm in the late 1880s, when it was auctioned and bought by Edwin Henty. The Henty family held it for many years, with Charles Lower the tenant, a poultry farmer, continuing into the new Century.

The smaller farms
In the 17th Century the Bennett family had also owned 'Upper Hangleton' or 'Highdown Hill' farm. In 1712 it passed to the Tidie family, and then by marriage to John Olliver (the eccentric Miller). By this time (1734) it was 8 acres. By 1836 it had passed to his grand-daughter Mrs Simmons and had grown to 20 acres. Her executors sold it in 1856 to Sarah Duke, who converted it to a freehold and sold it back to the Olliver family in 1858. Edwin Henty bought it 1866. The Penfold family farmed it from 1863 until, and well beyond, the end of the Century.

Another small farm which came into Henty's possession was Franklins Green Farm. In 1840 it belonged to Hugh Ingram; the tenant was William Knowles who also farmed the Bennett land. Edwin Henty bought it in 1845 and Thomas Meetens was farming 23 acres as his tenant there in 1851, followed by his son Reuben in 1866. Reuben Meetens continued until 1906, when he retired. The Sale of the Live and Dead Stock (equipment) showed this to be a mixed farm with dairy, poultry and arable.

One farm that stayed completely outside the Henty ambit was North Down Farm. The north-facing slopes of Highdown in the north of the Parish were split, with the western two-thirds a freehold, owned by the Shelley family in the 17th Century (and later by the Duke of Norfolk, who bought up much of the Shelley estate), and the eastern third in copyhold tenancies of the Manor of Ferring. The Norfolk portion, 50 acres including North Down Farm and its farm house, was farmed by the Olliver family in the 1830s and 1840s and the Piper family in the 1850s and 1860s. The eastern section was held by the Richardsons in 1800 and (by now 30 acres) was bought by David Lyon in 1835. The tenant in 1841 was David Page. It later became part of the Goring Hall estate.

Crops and livestock
The 1801 Census gives details of land use. Ferring had 311 acres of wheat, 196 of barley, 125 of oats, 60 of peas and 70 of turnips (this category usually included rape but in Ferring it would have been turnips, grown mainly for winter feed for sheep). The remaining 300 acres included pasture, meadows, and a little woodland in the north-west corner.

The field crops would have been grown in rotation, and yields were always good but falling wheat prices after 1870s prompted some small farmers to go into poultry farming, fruit growing, market gardening and horticulture. The railway made it relatively easy to sell these products in the London markets. One of the earliest ventures was Florence Villa, off Hangleton Lane, with a large orchard shown on the 1876 map (left), in what had previously been arable fields. Before that James Belchamber was listed as a Market Gardener in the 1874 directory, and George Sparkes in 1878. By 1882 George and Charles Penfold, at Upper Hangleton Farm, and Thomas Eyles at Florence Villa are listed in the Street Directory as Market Gardeners.

We have a good inventory of Ferring's livestock in 1801 from the 'Defence Returns' – a report of the parish's manpower and makeshift weapons that could be deployed against an invading French army, and the people and livestock that would need to be evacuated. This included 5 fatting oxen, 23 cows; 11 steers, heifers and calves; 8 colts, 562 sheep, 1 lamb, 110 hogs, 31 sows, 109 pigs. 6 riding horses, 12 waggons, 18 carts, 32 draft horses, and 10 draft oxen (for pulling ploughs).

In 1836 Edwin Henty advertised his entire 'live and deadstock' for sale because he was 'quitting' farming and letting his farmland out to tenants. The livestock comprised 700 sheep, 29 rams, one milking cow, and '23 powerful carthorses'; his 'deadstock' included 12 ploughs, 20 harrows, a portable 'thrashing machine', waggons, dung carts and many other items used in arable farming. It is not known whether the animals and farming equipment was bought by the incoming tenants.

Employment
For most of the century the only employment in Ferring was on the farms, in service, or self-employment as a craftsman. In 1801, the Miller must have been as much a businessman, buying grain and selling flour, as a craftsman but the mill had closed by 1827. The 1831 Census noted the occupation or social status of the inhabitants of each district, although without individuals' names. Ferring had five farmer-employers, 44 agricultural labourers, nine craftsmen or retailers, one 'capitalist or professional', and four 'others'. The retailer was probably Thomas Winton, of The Ramblers, because the Parish Register records his occupation as 'Shopkeeper' at the Christening of his son in 1815. The 'capitalist' was presumably Edwin Henty, as a banker, and among the 'others' may have been the Vicar, Francis Whitcombe. But this category cannot have included the servants – there were 28 of these in the 1841 Census.

Those described as 'servants' in the censuses often included those doing agricultural work as well as domestic service but the 1841 Census showed 35 labourers and 28 servants. There were two 'professionals' - Edwin Henty, listed as a banker, and Henry Dixon, the Vicar (they employed nine servants between them), and seven tenant farmers, some of whom employed indoor servants as well as farm workers. There were also 13 craftsmen – five shoemakers, three carpenters, two joiners, a sawyer, a stone mason, a bricklayer (all these either self-employed or working in a family enterprise) and a sailor. There were blacksmiths working in the village for most of the Century but none listed as resident in the censuses.

This broad pattern continued in the later censuses but with the addition of a few more 'professionals' (a surgeon, Dr Newton Hanson) some retired gentry and others 'of independent means'; and some non-manual occupations, such as postmen, shopkeepers, inn-keepers, railwaymen and teachers. It is noticeable too that the farm workers' occupations were recorded as more specific roles such as 'shepherd', 'cowman' and 'carter', and that (market) 'gardener' began to appear as a census occupation category.

The 1830s
The farm labourer's work was poorly paid, insecure and arduous. In the 1830s low prices for agricultural produce led to low wages or unemployment for farm labourers and there was unrest all across Sussex (the Swing Riots). There were no riots or criminal damage in Ferring but in the next parish, East Preston, Edmund Bushby was convicted of rick burning in 1830 and hanged at Horsham. He had rejected a low piece-rate for hand-flail threshing offered by the local farmer George Oliver, who threatened to use his threshing machine instead. Bushby was

later overheard saying, 'If I can't have my work by day, I'll have it at night', and there was circumstantial evidence that he and his brother stood and watched Olliver's haystack burn down. It is clear though that he acted alone, or with his brother, as an act of retaliation for unfair wages, not as part of any 'Swing' campaign of machine breaking.

There was also unrest in Goring in 1834. The Brighton Gazette reported on 6 November:

> The spirit of discontent among the rural population of this county has, we regret to find, already commenced in this neighbourhood. The price of wheat having declined to the ruinous sum of £9 and £10 per load, the wages have in consequence reduced, though not by any means in proportion to what flour can now be purchased at, and it is a fact that 10s a week at this time will buy more provisions than 12s would at the same time last year. On Monday last the farm labourers in the parish of Goring struck for higher wages, and obliged those who were unwilling to follow their example to leave their work, using threatening language to enforce arguments; in consequence the ploughs and teams were all deserted, and it appears as if the principle of the Trades Unions was about being established, for a very large assemblage of the labourers took place upon High Down Hill, a commanding eminence, overlooking the parishes of Goring, Ferring, Angmering, Tarring, &c.
>
> At this moment affairs assumed an unpleasant aspect; the farmers and occupiers immediately waited on Captain Pechell, at Castle Goring; and decisive measures were taken to frustrate any of the attempts that were made during the disturbances in 1831 and 1832. Warrants were issued, and informations taken against those who had forced others to leave their master's service and his property in danger, and the land occupiers have agreed to discharge all those who voluntarily absconded and joined the mob, and to call in aid and assistance from the adjoining parishes. The labourers, after meeting early on Tuesday morning, soon after separated, and it is to be hoped that the usual quiet will be resumed, as it is clear that the display of their meeting on High Down Hill, to cause the other parishes to join, proved a signal failure. The Earl of Surrey's corps of yeomanry, as well as the mounted guard, were all ready for giving assistance at a moment's notice, which gives great security to all property in that part of the country'.

One Goring farm labourer, George Ede, was given six months hard labour for leaving his work and joining the crowd on Highdown.

Later decades
Farm work was always poorly paid and sometimes dangerous. In 1840 a nine year-old boy from Ferring, James Collins, was driving a dung cart pulled by two horses, when they bolted. In trying to stop them he was thrown to the ground and run over by the heavy cart. He died within half an hour. William Bennett, a farm labourer of 71, was caught in a threshing machine in one of Edwin Henty's barns in February 1867. One witness was another labourer aged 13; another was an older man who told the Inquest that he had 'seen Bennett's head go round twice before we could stop the horses [that worked the machine] … The back part of his head was greatly injured from coming into contact with the stone floor of the barn'.

But there was little the labourer could do to improve his lot. His cottage was tied to his employment so it was very difficult to seek a better job without risking his family's home. Nevertheless it is clear that some farm workers managed to do this because the names in the successive Census returns show less continuity than one would expect. In some market towns in England annual 'Hiring Fairs' were held but there is no record of them in Sussex. However, in Ferring Henty's farm workers always benefited from the opportunity to stay in Ferring and work for Cortis and Richardson (later Lyon) and vice-versa.

Many families did stay: craftsmen handed on their trade to sons, some labourers rose to better-paid work on the same farm, or even farming on their own account (as did George Penfold) and at least one went on to be a shop keeper (Thomas Winton, his occupation as recorded as early as 1815, at the christening of his son). Some young men went into the Army, Navy or Merchant Navy, Surprisingly for a coastal village, none are recorded as fishermen, although the difficulty of mooring boats on a shingle beach may have been a factor.

As we have seen above, a labourer's working lifespan was from 9 to 70 or more (in the 1851 Census the occupation of one 8 year-old boy was recorded as 'Agricultural Labourer'). There was no question of retirement, unless supported by their children. Craftsmen too worked as long as they were able: John Moore was still making shoes at the age of 90. And work was six days a week and no holidays other than Christmas day and perhaps Good Friday.

The craftsmen were self-employed but some of them were very dependent on the agricultural economy- the blacksmiths, for example (we know the names of several of them, although none were listed as residents of Ferring in the Census lists between 1841 and 1901).

The First Shops
The first shop in Ferring was probably 'The Ramblers', the house in Church Lane that backs onto the churchyard, which Thomas Winton had bought in 1808. As noted above, he described himself a Shopkeeper, but the 1841 Census describes Winton as an Agricultural Labourer, and it may therefore have been his wife and daughter that ran the shop. The 1851 Post Office Directory lists him as 'Shopkeeper' and in 1855 as Shopkeeper and Postmaster, likewise the 1861 and 1862 Directories. The 1881 Census gives his wife's occupation as 'Grocer's Assistant', and the 1886 Street Directory again shows Mr Winton as the Postmaster. No doubt the shop was still operating at that time.

The 1845 Directory shows Thomas Hide, 'Beer shop and shoemaker' and John Moore, 'Beer retailer and shoemaker'. Hide must have been selling from his house, now known as Smuggler's Cottage'. John Moore was probably doing the same but by 1851 he had been installed at the recently opened 'New Inn'. The 1851 Directory also lists Miss Eliza Moore (John's niece) and Mr William Roots as 'Shopkeepers'. The 1851 census shows Eliza Moore as a 'Grocer and Baker'.

The 1862 Directory also names a Mr Cranstone as a 'Shopkeeper' – there is no address but we know that William Cranstone acquired Landalls Cottage in 1864, and that he married Eliza Moore between 1851 and 1861. They are both listed as 'Bakers' in the 1861 Census but Winton and Cranstone were shown as 'Shopkeepers' in the 1862 Directory. William Roots was shown in the 1851 census as a 'Woodman', probably living north of the railway, but we have no other information on him, or what he might have sold in his shop.

Peter Tourle is listed in the 1895 Directory as 'Baker, Grocer etc, Post Office'. He had taken over the premises (Holly Lodge) and the postmastership from Frederick Horner, some time after 1892, and presumably saw the opportunity to sell bread and groceries from the same counter. Sidney Wesson is listed as a shopkeeper in the 1895 Directory, and in the 1901 Census as a widower, living at 'The Shop' with his son Harold. They both give their occupation as Bakers. The shop was at 'Landalls', in Ferring Street, opposite the 20th Century Village Hall, and it continued as a shop, selling bread and much else, run by the Wesson family, into the 1940s.

The house now known as 'Smugglers Cottage', Ferring Street, in about 1895

The old Post Office in Holly Lodge, and Church Cottage,. Church Lane early in the new Century

CHAPTER 3: POVERTY, CRIME AND PUNISHMENT

Paupers

Under the Elizabethan Poor Law, it was the responsibility of the Parish to relieve the poverty of those who had been born in the Parish – those who were not native were sent back to the parish of their birth. Relief could be given in a number of ways but residential establishments where the inmates could be put to useful work were seen as the most economical and most moral solution. An Act of 1782 allowed parishes to form a 'union' to share the cost and administration of a workhouse. Four local parishes, of which Ferring was one, set up the East Preston Union workhouse in 1792. The Poor Law Amendment Act of 1834 set up a national system of Union Workhouses on a similar basis, and eventually the East Preston Union conformed to the national rules, and covered the area of 19 other local parishes. The workhouse was rebuilt in 1872.

East Preston Union Workhouse in 1856 ©West Sussex Record Office PL/WG9/56/1/18

Ferring had relatively few paupers and sent even fewer to the Workhouse. In 1803 there were only five paupers there from Ferring, in 1815 only one. The 1881 Census shows only two Ferring-born inmates at the workhouse. Aged parents stayed with the working family if possible, and the parish preferred to maintain others by 'outdoor relief', temporary if possible but permanent where necessary. Some of these might end up in the Workhouse Infirmary.

The funds came from the parish 'Poor Rate', levied on all property owners and administered by elected Overseers. In 1803 there were 17 residents receiving 'parochial relief' at home; in 1813 there were 23 recipients. At the other end of the century, the 1901 census shows Charlotte Moore (daughter of the long-lived John and Jane) aged 70 as 'living on the parish', on her own, at home, and Abraham and Mary Windsor 82 and 85, again, living on their own. Abraham was shown as a shepherd in the 1891 Census.

The Church no doubt helped in other ways. We are told that 'in Henry Dixon's time [1832-1870] there was given from the Vicarage Barn on St Thomas' Day [21 December] a measure of wheat to the poor'. This was part of an old Sussex tradition of 'Gooding' at Christmas.

Petty Crime

Poverty drove many to crime – from poaching 'conies' (rabbits) and stealing chickens and ducks, to petty theft. There were of course more serious offences, including assault, robbery and smuggling but even the more trivial offences were punished with severity. At the Quarter Sessions at Horsham in July 1807 James Viney, a Labourer from Ferring, was convicted of stealing five hens eggs, value 2d, the property of George Henty. He had been committed for trial on 13 Apr 1807; now he was re-committed for another calendar month in the House of Correction and then to be discharged (a total of four months).

At Petworth in 1824, Stephen Mitchell, 19, a Labourer from Ferring was convicted of stealing one drake (value one shilling) and three ducks (value three shillings), the property of George Henty, and sentenced to three months hard labour. In 1844, the same Stephen Mitchell, labourer, 39, was charged with 'stealing, at the parish of Ferring, on the 29th day of May last, two hen's eggs, value 2d, the property of Thomas Trussler, his master. A former conviction was put in. Prisoner pleaded guilty, and was sentenced to four calendar months hard labour', reported the Sussex Advertiser.

In 1850, William Holmes (on bail) was charged with stealing on the 21st day of June last, at the parish of Ferring, half a bushel of boulders, value 1d, the property of John Eede Butt. Mr Johnson conducted the prosecution. One calendar month hard labour.

In 1855, Arthur Bower was charged with entering a copse owned by Edwin Henty and cutting underwood to the value of 2d. Thomas Trussler, one of Henty's tenant farmers, said in evidence: 'As I was going along to the meadow, where a party of tramps had a fire, I saw Bower come out of a copse, with 10 or 12 hazel twigs in his hands, The ends of them were white, as if very newly cut. … We suffer a lot from such people in our neighbourhood, as they cut the wood to make pegs and rakes to sell.' Thomas Winton, Constable for Ferring, said he had served the summons on Bower by reading it to him, 'knowing him to be an ignorant person.' The magistrates found the prisoner guilty and fined him 2d, plus £1 3s 5d expenses.

Bower was treated rather leniently. Tramps and other vagrants were usually treated like criminals. As late as 1892 a 'disreputable looking old woman' was convicted of begging for bread in Ferring. She said she was begging her way to Kent where she could get work at fruit picking. She was sentenced to seven days hard labour.

There were few cases of more serious crime, other than smuggling. In 1841 Richard Kemp was committed for trial for breaking his stepmother's arm, and in 1865 James West, aged 72 was convicted of assault on a young girl, Elizabeth Hollands, and sentenced to six weeks hard labour.

Smuggling

Smuggling was certainly a serious crime in law, and was often accompanied by serious violence (as had been recorded at Ferring in the previous century), but it had died out in the 1840s as import duties were reduced, and by 1860 a trade treaty with France practically equalised the price of spirits between that country and Britain. The last recorded case in Ferring was in 1839. As the Brighton Gazette reported it in November, 'An attempt was made to run about 50 tubs of contraband spirit ashore at Ferring Sluice, a little before noon on Sunday, when it was known that most of the Kingston Station would be at church. Intimation, however, reached the man on duty of what was going on and, an alarm being made, 41 tubs and three men – named Wicks, Green and Cheeseman – were captured. The tubs were previously sunk near the shore, with a line attached to a stone at low water mark'. The year before, the Sussex Advertiser reported (30 April) that '60 tubs were run at Ferring but the Coast Guard succeeded in seizing of half of the contraband, the parties themselves all escaped capture'.

Earlier, in February 1832 a county newspaper had reported, 'A run of smuggled goods was attempted, and partly effected at Ferring Sluice, in the port of Arundel, on the 6th instant. Lieutenant Woolven, chief officer of the Kingston Guard, seized the boat, and six half-ankers of brandy; and an officer of the mounted Guard seized one man, and one half-anker. The man was taken before the Magistrates of Arundel on Tuesday last, and convicted in the penalty of £100, in default of the payment of which he was committed to the County Gaol at Horsham'.

The best-known case related to smuggling was in 1817 when George Henty was charged with landing 300 casks of 'geneva' [gin] on the beach at Sea Lane and storing them in his barns. The details of this case and the subsequent trial of two of the 'witnesses' are given in Chapter 8. Their perjury was proved but the evidence given in the trials showed that there had indeed been a smuggling operation on that date, but not involving George Henty.

Oral tradition indicates that smuggling was widespread in Ferring in the first half of the Century. John Winton, aged 80, celebrated his diamond wedding in 1941.. The *Worthing Gazette* interviewed him at that time, shortly before his death. He said his father had been a smuggler, in his younger days, before John was born. 'The whole village used to do a bit. In fact from Lancing to Littlehampton, thousands of pounds worth of tobacco, silk and spirits were smuggled in annually. They used to farm by day and smuggle by night.' This must have been in the 1830s, or early 1840s because by 1851 Thomas was respectable - Henty's Coachman, and by 1855, Ferring's Constable. John Winton told the *Worthing Herald,* 'They hid casks of spirits in the village pond, and the farmers would hide bundles of silks in their barns behind the animal feed. John Winton also told two stories about him grandfather Thomas, running from the 'Preventive Officers' and his grandmother hiding a cask of brandy under her skirts during one search of the house]

John Moore, in an interview with the People's Illustrated Paper, on his 70th wedding anniversary in 1894 said he had been involved as a young man, that he and his brother had 'worked many a barrel of brandy ashore on dark nights'

Licensing offences
From 1830 a licence (costing two guineas) was required for the brewing and sale of beer. There were at least two licensed outlets in Ferring in 1845. Kelly's Directory lists 'John Moore, Beer retailer and shoemaker' and 'Thomas Hide, beer shop and shoemaker'. The double combination is interesting. John Moore was the first landlord of the New Inn (renamed the Henty Arms in 1927) but must have been selling beer from his house before that because the land for the New Inn was bought only in April 1845. Thomas Hide (good name for a shoemaker) may have had a licence in 1845 but not so in 1870, when he was convicted of selling beer from his house, without one. In this and another case in 1854 a policeman seems to have acted as an *agent provocateur* to obtain the evidence.

From 1857 all local police officers were bought into a new West Sussex Constabulary.

Destitution
Begging and homelessness were treated as crimes. An old notice (presumably a painted board)

stil attached to one of the cottages near the churchyard in 1894, threatened a public whipping to 'rogues and vagabonds' found in the vicinity. The notice must have dated back to the 18th Century. Public whipping for vagrancy was common in the 16th Century but by the mid-18th Century the punishment for vagrants was more likely to be removal to a House of Correction (something between a workhouse and a prison; there was one at Arundel), for six months hard labour, before being sent back to their own parish.

In the Vagrancy Act of 1743 rogues and vagabonds were defined as 'gatherers of alms under false pretences; common players unauthorized by law and minstrels and all those wandering abroad, or those who pretended to be gypsies, and those playing or betting at any unlawful games; persons who ran away leaving their wives and families chargeable to the parish; unlicensed petty chapmen and pedlars; persons wandering abroad and lodging in alehouses, barns and outhouses and not being able to give a good account of themselves'.

Ferring had not had a particular problem with vagrants, perhaps only a dozen cases in the 18th Century of paupers removed to another parish, who may have spent some time in the House of Correction. It is interesting to wonder why the notice was put up. It may have been put up, or left up, as a warning by the Overseers of the Poor, to discourage claimants for relief.

Beggars were still dealt with very harshly at the end of the 19th Century, On 14 May 1892 the Sussex Express reported: 'Rebecca Sinns, a disreputable-looking old woman, was brought up in custody charged with begging at Ferring on Saturday. The woman said she had been in the Union [Workhouse] four times, and was begging her way to Kent, where she said she could get a job at fruit picking. She had a daughter at Brighton. She did ask for a bit of bread. It was shown that the policeman found bread and meat on her: she was sentenced to seven days' hard labour.

The poor and the homeless leave little trace in local history: no headstones in the churchyard, only the occasional entry in the Parish Registers of baptisms and burials – 'a tinker's child', 'a beggar woman', 'a tramp name unknown'… 'a man found dead in a field'. In this latter case the emaciated corpse was found in 1893, in a cornfield off Sea Lane. He had been there at least a week, the inquest was told, and rats had nibbled at his face. All he had in his pockets was a pipe and three pence.

The Workhouse as rebuilt in 1871-72, with a rather more forbidding exterior.

Reproduced by kind permission of Peter Higginbotham)

CHAPTER 4: THE CHURCH, EDUCATION AND PUBLIC SERVICES

The Church

St Andrew's Church was at the heart of the village in many senses. The old Manor House (Ferring Grange) was built next to it in the middle ages and the oldest cottages in the village are within yards of it. The farmers and labourers in Hangleton, Franklins Green and East Ferring, as well as those living in the central area, were in church there every Sunday for services as well as for christenings, weddings and funerals (it was also the parish church of Kingston until 1913). It was a social centre, and to some extent of local administration, as well as a place of worship.

St Andrew's Church 1851. Artist unknown.

The turret housing the single bell was added in 1792. The Victoria County History (vol V pt 2) tells us the Ecclesiastical Commissioners paid for restoration work on the chancel in the 1870s and in 1876 Edwin Henty spent £1,300 on a major restoration of the nave (which included a new roof and the rendering of the exterior walls) and rebuilding of the porch. He spent another £2,000 in 1887 on more restoration. And the new roof became infested with death-watch beetle and was replaced, at his widow's expense, in 1893.

Clergy

The Vicars of Ferring (who were also Vicars of East Preston) tended to serve for long periods – some of them practically a lifetime. James Penfold was Vicar from 1766 to 1812 (and also Vicar of Goring from 1770 until his death in 1812): Francis Whitcombe, 1812 to 1832 (also 'Perpetual Curate' of Lodsworth all that time); Henry Dixon from 1832 to 1870; Gregory Pennethorne 1870 to 1886, and Arthur Deane 1888 to 1918. The only exception in the 19th Century was the Reverend Robert Blight (1886 to 1888), who was arrested outside the village inn, drunk, at 7.30 one morning. He resigned immediately, after only 20 months in post. He had been the Diocesan Schools Inspector since 1872. Although no explanation was offered for his conduct it can be seen from the Parish registers that he had buried his wife, aged 43, nine months earlier.

There was usually a Curate, and we have the names of some of them. Richard Jones served for several years, before moving to a well-paid curacy in Kent in 1822. He went on to be an influential academic economist. J G Calhoun served 11 years in that capacity before being appointed Vicar of Goring in 1832. From 1864 the Curates were attached to St Mary's Church, East Preston. Most of the Curates served less than four years before moving on but Samuel Walker served 12 and William Nightingale, appointed in 1889, served 11.

Richard Jones - 1830s
National Portrait Gallery

Henry Dixon had the longest tenure of the 19th Century vicars. He was born in Sullington in 1798, son of the Vicar of Storrington. After Eton and Brasenose College Oxford he was ordained and took a post as a Curate at his father's church.

He was a Curate at St Paul's Church in Worthing from 1822 to 1832, and in 1829 he helped his brother Frederick set up the Ann Street Dispensary, forerunner of Worthing Hospital. He continued to live in Worthing, with his widowed mother until she died in 1835, and then moved into the old Vicarage in Ferring.

Rev Henry Dixon and Anne Dixon, outside the Vicarage, Ferring, 1863

In 1837 he married Anne Austen, cousin to Jane Austen. She had a strong interest in photography and natural history and, with a friend, Anna Atkins, produced an illustrated *Encyclopaedia of British Algae* in 1843, using an early system of photographic printing known as the Cyanotype, or Blueprint. This may have been the first-ever book printed with photographs. The Dixons had no children: she died in March 1864, not long after this photograph was taken.

His death, in 1870 was a little bizarre. A Sussex newspaper reported from the inquest that 'the rev. gentleman was sometimes a little strange, as he had asked after the health of Mrs Dixon on the day before his death, although she had been dead six years'. He went to bed in his normal health and was heard moving about at 11pm but his servant found him dead in the morning, 'lying by the side of the bed, on the floor. He was huddled up, with his mouth on the ground, his arm extended, and his hand clutching firmly the bed curtain'. The inquest concluded that it was from natural causes. He left no will and all his property went to his surviving brother.

The Vestry Committee

For most of the 19th Century responsibility for 'local government' was shared between the County Magistrates (highways, policing, licensing) the Manor Court (land tenure and agricultural regulation), and the Parish Vestry (local roads, relief of poverty and collection of the rates) The Vestry Committee was open to all ratepayers, chaired by the Vicar and administered by the Parish Clerk. It also had ecclesiastical duties, including the appointment of the churchwardens, the upkeep of the church and of the Vicarage, and the supervision of charities. We have already mentioned the distribution of wheat on St Thomas' Day. Lillian Candlin says in her book 'Tales of Old Sussex', 'The giving of these St Thomas' doles and other money collected in church for this purpose was stopped by the Ecclesiastical Commissioners in 1853 but in 1863 there was a Special Collection 'For relief of distress in manufacturing districts' - £9 collected at St Andrew's, plus £11 collected at East Preston church (at 2022 values, £1200 and £1400)

In Ferring the road responsibilities were carried out by the Waywarden in the 1840s and by Highways Overseers in the 1880s. The relief of poverty was financed by a Poor Rate, spent on contributions to the East Preston Union workhouse, maintaining a few paupers in their own homes and, after 1873, payments to the Village School.

Education

Some teaching may have been given by Ferring clergymen in the 18th Century, and there was a Sunday school in 1844 with a paid teacher and 12 pupils. The Sunday School was still running in 1872, when the Vicar, Rev. Gregory Pennethorne granted a corner of his Glebe land, just north of the Glebe Farm buildings in Ferring Street, for the building of a day school for the village children who were not receiving any weekday education.

There was already some weekday education going on in Ferring at this time. The Victoria County History volume says there were three 'dame schools' in 1818, 'one with 20 boys and girls in 1833, and two with 18 around 1846; up to 24 children receiving some schooling in 1851 and over 50 in 1871'. In 1878 'E.R.' (Emma Ree) was advertising her 'small, residential Seaside School for Young Ladies' at St Maurs. Jane Birt, aged 50, described herself as School Mistress in the 1851 Census, and was still in the same occupation in 1861 and 1871. She may well have been involved in all these schools. The dame schools probably closed down when the new school opened: there were no schoolteachers listed in the 1881-1911 Censuses other than Ellen Laker at the Village School (the 'National School 'as it was named on the 1876 Ordnance Survey map).

'National Schools' were those founded, or taken over by The National Society for Promoting the Education of the Poor in the Principles of the Established Church. It is not clear whether the Ferring School was founded by the Society or independently by the Vicar. He certainly gave the land from his Glebe, and managed the school with his churchwardens. In any event, the 1870 Education Act required all local authorities (in this case, the Parish Vestry) to report on the extent of provision of education to all 5 to 13 year-olds and provide for any shortfall. The schools provided might be supported by grants from the Government but were expected to be largely financed by the parish (if necessary from the Poor Rate) – and the pupils' parents were expected to pay few pence a week. Attendance was not compulsory until 1880, and not free until 1891.

Twenty-five children were admitted to Ferring's school when it opened in January 1873. The first teacher, Charlotte McIlwain, noted, 'On examining them, I found that, owing to there never having been a proper School in the village, they were very backward in writing and arithmetic; and also wholly undisciplined'. Charlotte did not stay long: she was followed by

Caroline Russell in 1875, Eliza Dredge in 1876, and Ellen Laker in 1880. But Ellen made her home in the village and continued as headmistress until 1919, when she was 60.

The school building was very small, just a single room 25 feet by 16, until it was enlarged in 1903.

A Centenary booklet has more extracts from the school records. The children used paper for the first time in March 1873 (previously they had used slates). In November 1882, one of the children swallowed a pencil and had to be sent home. On May Day 1884, ten children came in very late – one of them 'in a noisy manner and almost intoxicated, having spent some of his garland money on beer.'

Other public services
There were hardly any public services in Ferring (or the rest of the country) for most of the 19th Century. Church of England Elementary Schools like Ferring's could be supported by public expenditure after 1870, the destitute were eligible for admission to the workhouse or support in the community from parish funds, and the workhouse infirmary provided some minimal support for any really sick people who could not be cared for at home. The Overseers of the Parish supported these services from the Poor Rate. Any other form of personal support had to come from the family, from the church or from charities.

Public administration was minimal. There were Local Boards of Health in towns from 1848, responsible for public health, clean water and sanitation, but not until 1875 were there any comparable bodies in rural areas. In that year the East Preston Union took on these responsibilities, which were transferred in 1894 to the new Rural District Council. The Council's Medical Officer had jurisdiction in Ferring but there was no public water supply or sewerage until the 1930s,. Water came from wells with buckets and chains or hand-cranked pumps and sewage was disposed of in cess pits or 'earth closets'.

The village roads and the two small bridges over the Rife were maintained by the Parish Vestry until 1894. Only one 'main' road ran its short distance through Ferring – 'Herstle Street Lane', later known as Littlehampton Road. There had been a proposal in 1825 for new turnpike (toll) road running from Worthing, along the coast through Ferring (roughly along the line of the present Beehive Lane) to Rustington but this was not taken up. In 1889 the new West Sussex County Council took on responsibility for the Broadwater to Littlehampton Road.

There was a police service, of a sort, even in the early years of the Century. 'Village Constables' were appointed by the Manor Court until 1842 and then by Arundel Magistrates, with a staff of office and certain limited duties. It was not a full-time occupation: payment was by fees for particular actions such as serving a summons.. The Constable for Ferring in 1855 was Thomas Winton (Edwin Henty's coachman in the 1851 Census). The West Sussex Constabulary was formed in 1857, with full-time officers and it was another 90 years before Ferring had another resident police officer.

The national 'penny post' service was introduced in London in 1840 and quickly spread to the rest of the country. Ferring had a postmaster from at least 1845, Thomas Winton again, who also kept the first village shop, both services housed in 'The Ramblers' in Church Lane. He was still the Postmaster in 1887, at the age of 71. For all this period the service was purely 'at the counter': all mail had to be taken there for dispatch and collected from there when it arrived. The mail was brought to Ferring Post Office from Worthing, by horse until 1889, when it was switched to the railway. After Winton (died 1888), the Post Office moved across the road to Holly Lodge (initially under Frederick Horner, then under Peter Tourle), and stayed there well beyond the end of the Century.

By this time there were household deliveries, indeed three times a day. This old photograph shows four local postmen, serving East Preston., Ferring and Angmering c. 1904.

Manor Court

The Manor Court had always been mainly concerned with the regulation and registration of tenancies granted by the Lord of the Manor and to some extent with regulating common resources such as roads, bridges, ditches and hedges and this continued into the 19th Century. The Court met at Easter and Michaelmas (September) every year, in the Manor House (Ferring Grange), with the Bishop's Steward presiding, and by now, for the most part, simply had to decide on the 'admission' of new tenants to the various farms and cottages of which the Bishop was the landlord, whether by sale or inheritance. This included the transfer of tenancies in Fure, the small outlier of the manor, near Billingshurst. Increasingly, the sales or successions happened 'out of court' and the assignment of tenancies was a formality (on payment of the appropriate fee) but the copies of the entries on the Court Roll were proof of tenants' rights. Sub-tenancies and mortgages on copyhold property were also recorded on the Court Roll but leases such as those of the Henty family for the Bishop's own estate were granted or renewed directly by the Bishop and were not within the jurisdiction of the Manor Court.

In May 1832 the Court confirmed a list of 'Customs of the Manor'. Most important was the rule that daughters could inherit copyholds and that widows could continue their husbands tenancy as long as they remained 'sole and chaste'. Tenants who come to Court should get a good hot dinner and 'hay for their horses that come from Fure – gratis. Fure to do only fourth part of Beacon Watch'. Tenants had the right to 'to shrid the trees and hedgerows for frith and fuel and also the trees that overhang their corn and pasture land'. They also had the right ('free boot') to use timber on their land for gates, fences, carts and agricultural implements.

From 1852, changes in land law made it possible for tenants to 'enfranchise' their holdings (convert them to freeholds) and therefore take them out of the Court's jurisdiction. Many tenants did this and the importance of the Court declined.

New Local Government bodies

An Act of 1888 established County Councils in England and Wales, with administrative powers and duties transferred from the County Magistrates. The historic divisions of East and West Sussex were recognised for this purpose and West Sussex County Council became operational in April 1889. The Councils' most important function was the maintenance of highways and bridges: it was not until 1902 that they were given responsibility for education; and much later for social services. The only impact on Ferring would have been a disputed issue of responsibility for Horstlestreet Lane (later 'Littlehampton Road'), the only contender for 'County' status.

Local Sanitary Authorities were established under the 1872 Public Health Act and their powers were transferred to elected District Council by the 1894 Act. The East Preston Union had these responsibilities before 1894 and they were taken over by the new, elected, East Preston Rural District Council, The 1894 Act also established elected Parish Councils, mandatory for populations over 300 and available for those between 100 and 300, where an annual Parish Meeting requested it. Ferring held these meetings from 1895 but did not request a Parish Council until 1919.

CHAPTER 5: SOCIAL LIFE AND SPORT

Social life in Ferring, as everywhere else in Britain, was largely determined by social class. The gentry (the Hentys, the Vicars, the latter-day inhabitants of St Maurs, East Ferring House, and one or two other 'residences') only engaged with the farmers (their tenants) on rare public occasions, and even less with the tradesmen, agricultural labourers and servants.

Sport, for example, was a very small part of life in Ferring for the agricultural labourers and servants who made up the bulk of the population. The only organised sport they would have seen was cricket, played against other local villages. Other sporting activities like hunting and shooting were confined to the gentry, while their ladies played croquet. The farmers may have been too busy, or preoccupied, to join in village activities of this kind but we know that they took pride in their agricultural achievements and relished their successes in the County shows, sheep-breeding being a particular speciality.

Cricket

Agnes Henty was a niece of Edwin Henty, the owner of Ferring Grange, and of much of the village, when she was staying there in July 1864. She wrote in her diary for Friday the 22nd: *Started at about 12 o'clock for Arundel Castle with Papa, Aunt & Beta. Went & returned by train. Explored the keep, chapel, park, lake & dairy. Came home by 5 o'clock. Watched the cricket match between Ferring & Kingston in the field & after dinner to the races & other festivities.*

And Richard Standing, the historian of East Preston tells us: 'In July 1858 as part of a purely social occasion, George Olliver staged a cricket match between Ferring and Kingston clubs in his park at Kingston House. Guests included the Vicars of Angmering and Ferring, and Mr Wilkinson of the Lamb Inn, Angmering providing the repast, after which 'song and sentiment' flowed until eleven in the evening. Ferring won the match.

He says, 'Cricket matches involving East Preston are [frequently] reported from 1868 with games against Ferring. Before the modern weekend it mattered little on what day such events took place, barring Sunday which was sacred. Tuesdays, Fridays, and Mondays were favoured but for no obvious reason. A feature of the early club matches is that they had two innings, but a long afternoon would have been sufficient for men who made hay with a scythe.

'The Ferring team was distinctly the strongest, with the young curate Rev. Morres exhibiting skill of a good school, and he was responsible for half their totals, while Preston had more even scoring, bolstered by Mr Peachey and the Reeks brothers, and it is to the credit of Preston that all but Peachey were genuine villagers'.

These matches were played by 'scratch' sides but 25 years later there was a Ferring Cricket Club, playing regular fixtures. The Worthing Gazette of 11 October 1893 reported on the Club's 'wind-up' match of the season a few days earlier, against Goring, and gave an analysis of its performance over the season. The names of some of the players are very familiar – Peter Tourle (wheelwright and Parish Clerk), Albert Cousens (Henty's bailiff). Thomas Deadman (Henty's gardener) and Albert Hills (Landlord of the New Inn).

Other Masculine sports

Although there was no hunt based in Ferring, several hunting groups rode over its fields. An advertisement for the sale or lease of East Ferring House in 1827 said, 'Sporting Gentlemen would find this situation a desirable one, as it is in the immediate neighbourhood of Col. Wyndham's hunt; and harriers are likewise kept.' The Brighton Gazette advertised on 14 December 1865, 'Mr Gaisford's harriers will meet at Ferring Grange on 16 December'. Harriers hunted hares from horseback. Beagling, which was also recorded, involved hunting hares and rabbits on foot with beagles, the short-legged hunting dogs.

The 1881 Census records a Huntsman and a Gamekeeper living at Woodland Cottages in Goring Woods. The Gamekeeper was still there in 1891 and 1901, along with a 'Whip to Hounds. These individuals probably worked for the Castle Goring estate, the western edge of which extended across Titnore Lane to the Ferring boundary. The Gamekeeper would have been there to look after the pheasants until they could be shot by the Somerset family and their guests. But Edwin Henty had a 'Rookery' in the grounds of Ferring Grange in the 1840s, again, no doubt for shooting and East Ferring House was advertised for sale as with access to the partridge shooting on the fields east of Sea Lane.

Croquet

Agnes Henty's diary shows her playing a great deal of croquet between 1864 and 1869 - with the family and visitors at Ferring Grange, and at Steyne Gardens, Worthing. One of the earliest photographs associated with Ferring is a family group, with the lady on the left holding a croquet mallet.

Unknown croquet group, 'At Ferring 1864'

Croquet at Ferring Grange c.1900   Charles Conder.

Archery

Agnes also mentions Archery several times. She 'shoots' in the grounds of Ferring Grange and is rather pleased when she scores well. She also watches an archery tournament in Steyne Gardens, Worthing, in 1864.

Social obligations

We see in Agnes' diary something of the Hentys' position at the head of Ferring society. Her uncle Edwin Henty snr is a Magistrate. She visits a blind man, she goes to church, she helps to entertain guests at lunch and dinner. She enjoys the company of her cousins, Edwin Henty jnr and Arthur Henty, and is impressed by their service in the Volunteer Battalion of the Sussex Regiment – in which Edwin eventually became a Major, and Arthur a Colonel.

In 1872 Edwin Henty's daughter Maria, married Stephen Fuller. The Chichester Express of 7 May noted that Maria had always been kind to the poor and showed great interest in the Sunday school at Ferring, and that 'her doings in the village were very agreeable'. The West Sussex Gazette gave many more details, emphasising the social position of the Hentys and reporting, in a very condescending manner, the efforts of the villagers to decorate the churchyard and the entrance to the Grange.

The New Inn

The 'New Inn' was built at some time between 1845 when the land was purchased and 1851 when it appears under that name in street directories and the Census. The land was left to Edwin Henty by his mother's will. Edwin sold it, in April 1845, to his brothers George and Robert who owned the Henty Brewery in Chichester and some 50 inns and alehouses in Sussex. The business had been acquired by their father in 1827. It merged with the Constable Brewery in 1921 and continued as 'Henty and Constable' until 1955. In 1927 the company changed the name of their Ferring public house to the 'Henty Arms'.

The New Inn at the end of the Century

It has been suggested that the 'New' Inn was so named to distinguish it from an older inn but there is little evidence of such an inn. *Ferring Past* (Kerridge and Standing 1990) conjectures that the house now known as Franklands Manor near the northern end of Ferring Street fulfilled this function, under the name 'The Carpenters Arms'. The only evidence for this is that a piece of land behind this building was advertised to be auctioned 'at the house of the Widow Holden bearing the sign of the Carpenters Arms in Ferring in the county of Sussex', on 8 March 1783. Her husband had indeed been a carpenter and so was her son, so the sign might simply have been advertising their craft. And although the house was sold (14 years later) to Francis Sandham, a brewer, it was sold as a gentleman's residence not an inn, and there was no reference to any suitability for such a role. This would certainly have been a good position for an inn, just off the Broadwater to Littlehampton road, but there is no mention of it in the archives.

It is perhaps more likely that 'New' referred to a completely new facility in the village. The first innkeeper was John Moore. He had been listed in the 1845 Kelly's Directory as a 'Beer

Retailer and Shoemaker' (the latter was his lifetime trade); there was also an entry for 'Thomas Hide, Beer shop and Shoemaker'. In September 1870, the same Thomas Hide was convicted of selling beer, from his house, in glasses or pots, without a licence. John Moore presumably did have a licence (from 1830 a licence had been required to brew beer, or to sell it for consumption on or off the premises), and it would have been sensible to make him the landlord of the New Inn.

Most licensees did not stay long at the New Inn, and the early landlords may have continued to work at their own trade (as did John Moore, as a shoemaker). Exceptions were Thomas Gilliam (1866 – 1882) and Albert Hills (1888 – 1905). The New Inn was occasionally used for Inquests, for example one into the death of James Payne, found dead in a ditch in 'East Ferring Lane' in August 1890 (he had been drinking at that inn).

Public rejoicing
Queen Victoria's Golden Jubilee in 1887 was celebrated with a public dinner for 100 people, in a large tent in the grounds of Ferring Grange, The food and drink came from the Lamb Inn at Angmering and was paid for by Edwin Henty. A toast to 'The Queen of England and the Empress of India' was 'drunk with great heartiness, three ringing cheers being given. Other toasts of a complimentary character followed, and the company joined in the sports provided in the field through Mr Henty's liberality. The women and children were regaled with tea in the tent about five o'clock, about 200 sitting down', reported the West Sussex Journal on 21 June.

A similar event was staged for Victoria's Diamond Jubilee. This time the marquee was erected on 'the Cricket Field' (precise whereabouts unknown) and the catering was supplied by the Henty's own staff. Eighty men of the village sat down to 'a capital dinner'. Edwin Henty jnr this time proposed 'the Loyal Toast', the National Anthem was sung, hearty cheers were given and speeches were made about the Empire and the Queen's embodiment of its loyalty and unity. Once again, the women and children of the village were given a hearty tea, and this time there was a cricket match and a brass band.

Edwin Henty's funeral
Edwin Henty died in January 1890. Born in Ferring in 1805, he had lived all his adult life in the village and had built up the family bank from three to six branches in the county, and the family landholdings into almost three-quarter of the parish. He paid for substantial renovations to St Andrew's Church. He was a leading magistrate and was much involved in early local government.

Over 400 people attended his funeral in Ferring, including most of the notables of south West Sussex. But the Ferring residents turned out too, the Worthing Gazette reporting that, 'Blinds were drawn at the few cottages which lie near to the mansion of the departed gentleman, and the villagers, most of them in mourning attire, gathered in groups in the roadway and indulged in quiet converse'. Edwin Henty seems to have been genuinely popular as well as respected. The Gazette recalled that 'his golden wedding two years ago was made the occasion of much public rejoicing in the village, and that everybody from miles around had been invited to partake of the festivities'.

CHAPTER 6: BUILDINGS

Most of the notable buildings of 19th Century Ferring in the 19th Century were already old in 1801, and were still standing in 2022, although a few have been lost and a few altered considerably. There was little new construction from the 18th Century to the 1920s because the size of the population, and the wealth of the landowners, was restricted by the yield of the farmland.

St Andrew's Church

The church is of course the oldest building in the village. The bell turret was added in 1792.and the external appearance of the building has hardly changed since then. The turret was rebuilt in the 1870s, the walls of the nave were rendered in 1886. and the present lychgate was built in 1897, funded by popular subscription, to commemorate Queen Victoria's Jubilee.

St. Andrew's Church in 1810 – a sketch in The Gentleman's Magazine. Part of Ferring Grange behind, right.

Inside the church more extensive work was done in repairs and renovations, paid for by Edwin Henty snr. The ceiling of the chancel was raised and new pews installed in the nave in 1851. In 1875, more work was done on the chancel and in 1886 the nave was given a new roof and the some of the internal walls dismantled and rebuilt, Edwin Henty paying £2,000 for this and other remedial work. The full story is set out in the church guidebook (*St Andrew's Church in the village of Ferring:* 2017 edition).

Ferring Grange

Ferring Grange was the grandest house in the village but little is known about its development in the 19th Century. It had begun as the farmhouse of the Bishop's demesne in mediaeval times and that building was usually occupied by the leaseholder of the estate (and occasionally, we are told, by Bishop William Rede (1369-1385)) . It must have been extended – perhaps even rebuilt – several times by the late-16th Century, when it is mentioned in Thomas Waterfield's will. He allocates 'the great chamber and the kytchin' to his widow and the other two-thirds of the building to his son John. The 1621 plan of the Manor Estate shows a substantial house in a single north-south range, and two ranges of farm buildings. Thomas Cooper's inventory of 1751 indicates that the house then consisted of a garret, presumably in the roof, with six chambers or bedrooms, over six ground-floor rooms.

George Henty had taken over the house by 1800. His son Edwin had made improvements in 1840. A valuation of that year notes, 'The House which Mr Henty occupies has lately undergone some improvements. The Farm Buildings which immediately adjoined have been removed which has considerably improved the Appearance & Value of the Residence.'

It is difficult to say when the house assumed the appearance it had at the end of the Century. Edwin Henty senior acquired the freehold in 1864 and this would have been the earliest likely date for major changes. But his niece Agnes Henty does not mention any rebuilding in her diary record of her visits in 1864, 1867 and 1869, and the footprint of the house in the 1876 and 1898 Ordnance Survey large-scale maps looks very similar to that of the 1837 Tithe map (apart from the addition of a conservatory). The picture below is from a postcard sent in 1906 and

includes an extension of the south wing, which must have been added right at the Century's end. Perhaps there were other changes at that time because a guidebook, 'The Sussex Coast' by Ian Hannah (published in 1912) refers to 'Ferring Grange, a large modern house'.

There was a drive from Ferring Street (seen in this picture curving round to the main entrance). **Grange Lodge** was built in the late 1860s, for the coachman, at the Ferring Street end.

The other 'Residences'
Further up Ferring Street was the **Vicarage**. It had been rebuilt in 1783 for £89, but not to any high standard: some of the early-19th century vicars declined to live there. There were further changes in 1871, to suit the new vicar, leaving it very much as it appears now, except for the house built onto the northern elevation. The stables have gone and the coachman's cottage is now a substantial house.

The 'Topographer' magazine of 1790 reported that 'the Vicar has built himself an excellent square brick house nearly opposite the church', and this still surives as the core of 'Greystoke

Manor'. It was known as 'The Square House' until the 1840s when a wing was added, and from 1846 at least was known as '**St Maurs'**. After the Rev James Penfold, it passed to his son and then his daughter, who passed it on to her son (Edwin Henty). It was put up for auction in October 1834 as a 'Family Residence' and thereafter was owned by William Marshall (Henty's chief tenant farmer, who is listed with six servants in the 1841 Census), Major McPhail (1845-48), Newton Hanson (a Surgeon 1848-1857), and Mr Robert Hughes of Kensington (Gentleman, 1857-73). The Hentys bought it back in 1873 and it had a number of tenants up to 1892, when Edwin Henty Jnr and his wife occupied it for a few years before moving into Ferring Grange (where his mother continued to live until her death in 1897).

Home Farm House was built around 1810 for George Oliver Penfold, son of the Vicar, presumably as a Gentleman's Residence. The house passed to George's sister, Ann, and on Ann's death in 1832 to her son Edwin Henty. At some point in the 1840s Henty let it out to the tenants of his most important farm, and it became known as '**the Farm House**' (not *Home Farm House* until the 20th century). In the 1851 Census the tenant was John Golds, who was farming 450 acres (not all in Ferring). Between 1852 and December 1857 it was occupied by Samuel Saunders to whom Edwin Henty had leased the house along with the 208 acres of 'The Lower Farm'.

Edward Perronet Sells, a retired Coal merchant was probably the next tenant (of the house – Edwin Henty had now taken the Home Farm back 'in hand', managed by a Bailiff living in the original, more modest, farmhouse nearer the farm buildings). He stayed until his death in 1873, and the house was let to a Mr Cockburn . In the 1890s it was let to another 'Gentleman', Thomas Clarence, and his widow was living there, 'on her own means' as late as 1911.

The house now known as **Franklands Manor** may possibly have been an inn in the 1780s but when it was advertised for sale in 1828 it was as a 'dwelling house which might, at trifling expense, be converted into a very comfortable residence for a small genteel family'. It was never a manor house. Edwin Henty bought it, and a recently built terrace of six cottages, in 1830, to be occupied by his tenant (Thomas Trussler) and the labourers of his northern farm.

The only other house with any 'genteel' occupiers was **East Ferring House** in Sea Lane. Probably built in the 16th Century, it was a copyhold estate of the Manor of West Ferring and had no historical connection with East Ferring Manor. The Cortis family (large-scale farmers in Angmering and other nearby parishes) held it from the beginning of the Century until 1838, when it was sold to the Lyon family who had acquired large parts of Goring and East Ferring. They bought the freehold in 1876. Dr Clarke RN (who had been a prison governor) occupied the house from 1836 (possibly earlier) until his death in 1890. It was vacant at the 1891 Census but occupied in 1900 by Albert Hills, a tenant farmer (presumably on land in East Ferring owned by the Lyon family).

Farmhouses
If the occupiers of the 'residences' were the gentry, the tenant farmers described themselves (at least in the first half of the Century) as 'yeomen'. Probably the largest farmhouse in Ferring was the house we now call **Hangleton Grange**, probably built before the 17th Century, owned by the Bennett family until 1890, when it was sold to Edwin Henty. In the 19th century it was known as Hangleton Farm but it is easily confused with another, much smaller, farmhouse at the north end of Hangleton Lane, rebuilt in 1734 (from another 17th Century house), owned by another branch of the Bennett family. The old house was known as the **Upper House** and the

rebuilt one as **Hangleton, or Hangleton Grange**. What adds to the confusion is that the northerly part of what is now Langbury Lane was known as Hangleton Lane until the 1930s. Hangleton Grange was acquired by Edwin Henty in 1890, 'Hangleton' at the top of the lane in 1866; the Penfold family were living there and farming the land from 1863 until well into the next century.

Pledge's Cottage, now named **Elford House** in Ferring Lane was another 17th Century farmhouse, where the Sewell family had lived for at least three generations. It was a substantial house in 1649, as an inventory of that date shows. John Pledge, another Ferring Yeoman, took a 21 year lease on the property in 1773, and the farmhouse was shown as 'Pledge's Cottage' as late as the 1899 Ordnance Survey map. In 1810 it was acquired by John Cortis and, says *Ferring Past*, was separated from its farmland. In 1840 it belonged to the farmer Phineas Belchamber. He died in 1851 just before the Census and it is not clear who the owners and occupiers were thereafter. It served as two cottages for most of the century.

East Ferring Farmhouse, in Sea Lane had belonged to the Cortis family until 1839, when it was sold to David Lyon, who was buying up as much land as he could in East Ferring and Goring. James Cortis and then his son William Cortis continued to farm the land and live in the house until 1904 The house was demolished in the 1950s and the site formed the entrance to the new Midhurst Drive housing development.

Manor Farmhouse, just 200 yards further south on Sea Lane, was the base of Manor Farm, and historically, the Manor of East Ferring. By 1840 the farm was much reduced in size and owned by the last of the Westbrook/Richardson family who had been Lords of that very small Manor since the 17th Century but now lived in a grand house in Findon. It was used as two farm labourers' cottages from at least 1840 and until it was demolished in the early 1960s. The site was never built on and by the year 2000 was a copse with extensive and impenetrable undergrowth.

Manor Farm Cottages, just into the next Century

Franklands (or Franklins) Green Farmhouse was the base of the rather small (28 acre) farm acquired by Edwin Henty in 1845, The tenant in 1851 of the house and farm was Thomas Meetens, and his son Rueben followed him until he retired in 1906, aged 70.

North Downs Farmhouse, on the far side of Highdown, was the residence of the tenant farmers of the 1850s and 1860s but from the 1871 Census onwards, when the farm was part of a larger holding beyond the boundaries of Ferring, it was inhabited by farm labourers.

Isolated farm buidings

Most of the farm buildings were adjoining the farmhouses but there were a few isolated groups of farm buildings. notably in the south of the parish – what was described in the 1921 Sale Catalogue for Home Farm as ' stables etc'. In the 1920s it was known as Sea Barn, and then, after conversion to a house and then a school, as 'The Tudor Close', a fanciful name without any historical foundation.

There were some farm buildings close to the Vicarage, where the Library now stands. A large barn, reputedly 18th Century, was demolished in 1964. This must have been part of the Vicar's Glebe farm.

In the north of the parish were North Barn Cottages and a large barn (part of Henty's holdings) – still to be seen as 'Lansdowne Nursery' on the north side of Littlehampton Road.

The Cottages

The only other buildings in the village were the cottages of the farm labourers, a few workshops, the New Inn (from 1851), the Crossing Keeper's Cottage (from 1846) and the Village School (from 1873).

May Tree Cottage: sketch by Montague Penley (1799-1881)

Opposite the church stood the old houses we now know as Holly Cottage, Church Cottage and May Tree Cottage all dating back to the 17th Century or earlier. The first two looked very much as they do today. The next house, 'Erebus',is a modern in-fill. May Tree Cottage appears in a drawing by a 19th Century artist, mysteriously labelled 'Constable's House, Ferring'. There is no record of John Constable having lived in Ferring, painting any of its houses or even visiting the village, and it may be that the caption referred to the cottage in which the village constable lived (until 1857 this was a part-time officer appointed by the Arundel magistrates).

On the west side of the lychgate (rebuilt in 1897) was (and still is) the Ramblers, built in the 1790s. It belonged to the Winton family for most of the century and from 1845 was a shop and the village Post Office, until that service moved to Holly Cottage in the late 1880s. Note, in the picture opposite, the thatch on the

Eastern end of Church Lane: Church Cottage (left), the Ramblers and the former churchyard cottage (right) and The Old Cottage in the background, from a postcard

north-facing roof but tiles on the south, exactly as it is today. On the east side was a double-cottage building that was demolished in 1906 to allow an extension to the graveyard (the outline of the building can still be seen in the rectangular depression in the ground).

Round the corner from May Tree Cottage, there was the equally old Evergreen Cottage, abutting it . On the opposite side of Ferring Street was 'The Old Cottage', otherwise known as 'Barley Style Cottage'. Smugglers Cottage is a much later building but was recorded in the 1840 Tithe apportionment – not under that name, which would have been very provocative in the first half of the Century, when smuggling was still prevalent, a serious crime. There were two more cottages: Yew Tree (then known as 'Bushby's) and Woolvens, later known as Dairy Cottage. These, plus the Vicarage and its Glebe farm buildings, made up the nucleus of the old 'West Ferring' village

A 1930s picture of a scene unchanged from the 19th Century - labourers' cottages in Sea Lane.

The labourers from East Ferring Farm and Manor Farm lived in in the cottages strung out along Sea Lane, many of them former substantial houses like Whittingtons, Stocker's and Sluggards, converted to pairs of semi-detached houses, later known as Carisbrook, Bramble and Laburnum Cottages, Two of the three houses north of Laburnum Cottage had been built by 1837 as a single tenement but the most southerly one, later known as Fuller's Cottage, must have been built some decades later, certainly by 1876, when it appears on the Ordnance Survey map. A pair of cottages opposite East Ferring Farm (replaced by Homestead Cottages in the 1930s), and the Lodge at the Ferring end of the drive to Goring Hall, were also built in the 19th Century. Together with the two farmhouses and East Ferring House, they made up the settlement of 'East Ferring'.

CHAPTER 7: FAMILIES

The Hentys

The Henty family dominated the 19th Century in Ferring, and in much of south-west Sussex. An article in *The Topographer* in 1790 refers to **William Henty** (1731-1796) as the leaseholder of the main estate in Ferring– 'an opulent farmer from Littlehampton'. He was the son of John Henty of Littlehampton and grandson of another John Henty, who was married at Ford in 1695. William had bought the lease of the Ferring estate from the Shelley family in 1786 and shortly before his death in 1796 he obtained a new lease direct from the Bishop. In his will, made in 1794, he left his son, George, the Ferring lease and other property in Ferring, Billingshurst, Slinfold, Itchingfield and Chiltington. He left Thomas all his land in East Preston, Littlehampton and Rustington. Thomas seems to have sold some of these properties and bought Church Farm, Tarring soon after his father's death. He was particularly interested in farming and breeding sheep and sent his sons out to Australia in 1829 to explore the opportunities for sheep farming there. He followed in 1832. The family business prospered enormously in Tasmania, and then Victoria, and continued into the 20th and 21st Centuries.

George Henty (1766 -1829) certainly inherited much property from his father but he was a substantial businessman in his own right. He ran the Ferring estate successfully and started to buy up other land in Ferring from the copyholders. Then he branched out and, with his brother Thomas, founded the 'Henty, Henty and Hopkins Bank' in Worthing in 1808. By 1828 he had acquired a brewery in Chichester. He left this to his sons George and Robert Henty, both of whom had moved away from Ferring. George jnr, born Ferring in 1803, was mayor of Chichester in 1858.

George Henty's will left the Banking businesses 'now carried on by me in Co-partnership with Messieurs Luke Upperton, James Henty and Robert Upperton at Worthing, Arundel and Steyning in the said County of Sussex' to his son Edwin, born in Ferring in 1805. (the James Henty referred to was probably the younger brother of George snr).. The Henty Bank issued its own bank notes for £1, £2, £5, and £10.

Like his father, George Henty had married (1790) into a local property-owning family. His bride was Ann Penfold, daughter of the Vicar of Ferring. George and Ann Henty had five sons and seven daughters, born between 1790 and 1811. The eldest son, William, lived to a good age and died in York; the next son, James, became a mine owner and a stockbroker (and was the father of the Victorian author of boys' stories, G A Henty); the next was George, who became a Town Commissioner in Worthing; then Edwin, who inherited the Ferring estate; the youngest was Robert, who lived in Chichester and ran the brewery.

Edwin Henty 1803-1890 was the fourth of George' five sons. He took over the running of the bank, and of the Ferring estate – which, like his father, he augmented by buying up copyhold land and cottages. He also arranged exchanges of land with his neighbours in Ferring, so as to consolidate his holdings. In 1862 he began turning his leasehold and copyholds into freeholds, buying their 'enfranchisement' from the Church Commissioners who had taken over from the Bishop of Chichester as the principal landlords.

He married Laura Boghurst in 1839, and evidently made some improvements to Ferring Grange at that time, as noted in Chapter 4. He went on to substantially rebuild and extend the house considerably after he had acquired the freehold in 1864. The extent of his landholding in

Edwin Henty 1804-1890

Ferring is set out in Chapter 1, and the organisation of his farms in Chapter 2. He was a considerable benefactor to St Andrew's Church, giving over £3,000 between 1875 and 1887, for the restoration of the chancel and the nave.

His influence extended well beyond Ferring however. He was a Banker, with branches in Worthing and five other towns in West Sussex, a Magistrate for nearly 50 years – Chairman of the Bench at Worthing since 1868, a Worthing Town Commissioner, and Treasurer of other early local government bodies His bank financed much of the development of Worthing, and he formed a company in 1844 to build the line linking Shoreham to Chichester. This 'Brighton and Chichester Railway Company' was sold to the London and Brighton Railway as soon as the line was completed.

When he died, in 1890, his personal wealth was just under £150,000.

Edwin Henty jnr (1844-1916) was the elder of Edwin's two sons. He was sent to Rugby School and afterwards took up a position in the family bank. He was still living at The Grange in 1871 (occupation, 'Banker') but lived with his wife in Ifield (Crawley) from at least 1878 until after his father's death in 1890. In 1881 he was again listed as 'Banker' (perhaps managing the Crawley Branch). At the 1891 Census he was still living at Ifield. By 1895 he was living at St Maur's (now Greystoke Manor): his mother continued to live at Ferring Grange until her death in 1897. He and his brother sold the Henty Bank to Capital and Counties Bank in 1896 but he stayed on as a Director of the new bank.

He, Edwin, married Georgiana Laura Alma Henrietta Elizabeth Somerset (a descendant of the Duke of Somerset, and related to the Somersets of Castle Goring) at Hove in 1875. They had no children.

He does not seem to have added to the family land bank, and actually sold a few acres, but in the 1910 Land Tax assessments he was recorded as owning nearly 600 acres in Ferring, most of the large houses and some 25 of the 50 cottages in the parish. He did have wider interests however: he bred pedigree South Down sheep, was a keen gardener, and it was he who organised the first serious excavation of the Highdown Saxon Cemetery in 1890.

Edwin and Arthur were both part-time soldiers. Edwin joined the Volunteer Battalion of the Royal Sussex Regiment in 1864, reaching the rank of Major in 1890,

Mr Edwin Henty, V.D., J.P., D.L.

and was awarded the Volunteer Officer's Decoration (VD) for 'long and meritorious service'. He was appointed elected West Sussex County Council Alderman in 1890, appointed Deputy Lieutenant in 1902, and High Sheriff in 1903. He died on Christmas Day 1916, leaving £143,000, all to his widow.

Arthur Henty (born 1848) carried on the family tradition of going to Rugby School (between 1862 and 1865). He also went into the family bank, and was living at the Grange in 1871. On 11 July 1872 he married Louisa Curtis Hawes at St George's Church in Bloomsbury, London. They lived principally at Broadwater Hall, Worthing. He was also a Director of the Henty Bank and of the Capital and Counties Bank that took them over in 1896. In the next Century he had moved to Oaklands Park in the centre of Chichester, where he died on 29 December 1936. He was buried in Ferring Churchyard.

Arthur Henty 1848-1936

The Cortis family

The Cortis family had been farming in Ferring since the 17th Century. In 1801 **John Cortis** (1757-1838) owned much of the old East Ferring Manor (which included large plots west of Sea Lane) and East Ferring House. In his will he left large amounts of money in trust for his sister and nephews (he never married) with £100 for his surviving brother George. He left his 'household goods, furniture and effects, linen, plate, china, books, wines and liquors' to his five nieces. All his other property was to be sold and his nephew, another John Cortis, was to have the first opportunity to buy it. In fact, it was bought by David Lyon, who was building up his estate in Goring and East Ferring. – his Goring Hall was completed in 1840.

This nephew **John Cortis (1793 – 1866)** was the son of James and Catherine. His brother George Cortis was born in 1794. The photograph (left) which turned up a few years ago, is inscribed on the back, 'John Cortis of Ferring who departed this life May 10th 1866 aged 73 years'. He had married Mary Ellis Peters, at Angmering on 27 December 1828. They had twin sons James and William Peters Cortis, christened at Angmering on 22 September 1829. John did not buy his uncle's estate but occupied it as a tenant of David Lyon.. In the 1851 census he is described as a 'Farmer of 120 acres, employing four men and two boys'. He was still there in 1861 but by 1871 John was dead and William, still single at 41, was running the farm, with his widowed mother as housekeeper.

William P Cortis (1829 – 1904) married Elizabeth Miles in 1874, in Angmering. She was born in 1832 in Angmering, and came from the prosperous Miles family who lived and farmed at Upper Ecclesden Farm. In the 1881 Census he is shown as a farmer of 250 acres (almost certainly at East Ferring Farm). In 1901 he was living in East Ferring Farm House, in Sea Lane, still described as a farmer (although probably no longer farming), born in Angmering. He died in Ferring in 1904. Elizabeth died there in 1910.

The Bennett families

It is very difficult to work out the relationships between the 238 Bennetts who are recorded in the Parish Registers, especially since they so many of them shared Christian names, *Ferring Past* notes that the John Bennett who inherited the copyhold tenancy of Hangleton Farm (Langbury Lane) in 1801 was the son, grandson and great-grandson of three previous John Bennetts, and the father and grandfather of two subsequent John Bennetts. The last of these inherited in 1804. He farmed it himself until 1832 at least, but in 1840 and 1841 he was not living in Ferring, and the land was being farmed by a sub-tenant, William Knowles. By 1851 he was again farming it himself, listed in the Census as 'Farmer of 50 acres, employing three labourers'. The farm passed to his widow Charlotte, and then to their grand-daughter Fanny Cooke, in 1885. Fanny obtained the freehold and put it up for auction. It was bought by Edwin Henty.

That branch of the Bennett family seems to have died out but there were other Bennett families who were Agricultural Labourers, not landowners or tenant farmers. John Bennett had married Sarah Nye in 1789 and had ten children. His brother James married Ann Belchamber in 1807 and had nine children. By 1841 there were six Bennett families in Ferring – William aged 40, with three young children, James (28) with three children, Francis (35) with four children, James (55) with five children, George (40) with six, and Thomas (30) married but without children. All the men were Agricultural Labourers.

The Penfolds
There were probably two distinct Penfold families in Ferring in the 19th Century. James Penfold was the long-serving Vicar who died in office in 1812. He was a substantial landowner and had himself built a large house in 1791 initially known as The Square House, then as St Maurs, and in the 20th century as Greystoke Manor. His daughter Ann married George Henty in 1790. James' son George Olliver Penfold inherited in 1812, and on his death the estate went to his sister Ann, and thence to the Henty family.

The Penfolds who farmed were probably only distantly related, if at all. Charles Penfold and three others who might have been his brothers were listed as Agricultural Labourers in the 1851 Census but by 1861 George is listed as a Farmer, and in the 1891 and 1901 Census his son George is shown as a farmer at Upper Hangleton.

The Moores
There are Moores in the Parish registers from 1575 (one the Vicar of Ferring in the 17th Century) but in the 19th Century the family is known mainly for the long marriage of John and Jane Moore, whose lives practically spanned those ten decades. John was christened in Ferring church on 11 May 1804, was married there on 16 June 1824 and was buried there on 24 February 1895. His wife, Jane Stallard was born in Warblington in 1807, and died a few months after her husband. The couple had 13 children christened in St Andrews Church, and there were 41 granddchildren.

John's trade was cordwainer or shoemaker but he is recorded in the 1851 Street Directory as 'Beer Retailer', The Census of that year places him in Franklins Green and it is almost certain that he was first landlord of the 'New Inn'. He stayed there until 1858 and returned to his old house and shoemaker's shop in Ferring Street, next door to his wife's family. His wife and several of his children were also in the trade. John still described himself as a 'Bootmaker (Self-employed)' in the 1891 Census, when he was 86 years old.

John's brother George, some 15 years older than John, was a carpenter. His son George was also a carpenter but his daughter Eliza was described as a Grocer and Baker in the 1851 Census. She married William Cranston and they were listed as shopkeepers in the 1861, 1871 and 1881 Censuses.

John and Jane became more than local celebrities when the Vicar wrote this letter to the Times in 1894.

A SEVENTIETH WEDDING DAY.

TO THE EDITOR OF THE TIMES.

Sir,—There is in this village so remarkable a case of what may be called married longevity that I think it deserves notice in your columns. The registers of the parish record the baptism of John Moore on May 11, 1804, and his marriage to Jane Stallard on June 16, 1824. Both the old people are alive and well, and will consequently celebrate their 70th wedding day on Saturday next.

The registers also contain entries of the baptisms of their 13 children, beginning with Charles Stallard on May 11, 1825, and ending with Mary Anne on May 30, 1847. The eldest son is still alive, and I am curious to know if there is any one else as old as 69 who has both parents living.

Old Moore, who is a shoemaker by trade, has been a hardworking, steady man, and has much to say of past days. His stories relate chiefly to great takes of conger and other sea fish in which he has played his part, also smuggling (*quorum pars*, &c.), which was very prevalent on this coast in his younger days. He is one of the almost extinct race of small freeholders, and lives in the house his father owned before him. It is very picturesque, and not a little dilapidated, but will, I think, last his time. I trust the same may be said of the savings on which he is now living, as he can do little work, though he is proud of having soled a pair of boots on his 90th birthday. The old lady has evidently once been a beauty, judging from her present good looks, and is often seen in her place in church.

I propose to have a photograph taken of the venerable couple on their wedding day. This I shall be glad to send to any of your readers who may like to forward to me half-a-crown, and the profit shall be duly given to the deserving old people.

Yours faithfully,
A. M. DEANE, Prebendary of Chichester and Vicar of Ferring.
Ferring Vicarage, Worthing, June 9.

John and Jane Moore 1894, Rose Cottage, Ferring Street.
Photo by Walter Gardiner

The Vicar sent the photograph to the Queen and, in reply, had a note back from the Queen's Privy Purse Office, with a postal order for £3. In return he sent the photograph, which is still in the Royal Collection.

The letter refers to the smuggling that went on in Ferring in John's younger days and, in a Latin quotation, indicates that John had a part in it. John quite openly told one of the journalists who came to see him after the Times letter that he and his brother had 'worked many a barrel of brandy over Ferring beach'. John died in February 1895, Jane five months later. By that time they had 42 grandchildren.

The Tourles
The various branches of the Tourle family were noted in *The Day Before Yesterday: Ferring in the 20th Century*' but they have their place in the 19th Century too. William Tourle was born in West Grinstead, in 1832 (one of eleven children) and married Ellen Goldsmith at Goring Church in 1857. They lived for some years on a farm near Goring Station, but by 1864 they had moved to Lilac Cottage, Ferring (where 'Pump Court' now stands). William was a 'Carpenter', Ellen was a 'Laundress 'in the 1881 census and classed herself as an employer in the 1891 census. By 1901 she and her daughter Ada both classified themselves as 'Laundresses working on their own account'. William had died the previous year. They had eight children.

The fifth born was Peter Albert Tourle (1864-1959). who married Alice Kenchet in 1890. He was the village undertaker as well as carpenter and wheelwright. He also served as Parish Clerk from 1895 and Postmaster in 1900. They lived in one of the Franklands Cottages in Ferring Lane, before moving to Holly Lodge, where they had the Post Office. Their children were William H Tourle (1892-1930), Peter Albert Tourle jnr (1893- 1990), Sidney Tourle (who lived in Langbury Lane for many years) and five others.

The Wintons
This was another prominent family among the working community, all through the Century. Charles Winton married Sarah Hale, from an old Ferring family, in 1772. Their second son Thomas was born in 1774 married Jane Hide in 1798. In 1808 Thomas bought the recently-built cottage in Church Lane, later known as The Ramblers, for £105 (an odd sum in pounds but a nice round 100 guineas).It is not clear how he was in a position to pay such an amount (equivalent to £20,000 in 2022) but in 1815 Thomas' son George was baptised at St Andrew's Church, with the father's occupation recorded as 'Shopkeeper'.

Two years later, in 1817, Thomas Winton was involved in the smuggling case against George Henty. He said he was on the beach and saw it happen. Subsequently George Henty had the two main witnesses prosecuted for perjury and during that trial it was shown that Winton could not have been on the beach that morning. He admitted that he had 'been concerned in a smuggling transaction on the evening of that day but Mr Henty had no part in it'. It would seem that Winton was well known as a smuggler and that there was a plot to incriminate Henty as a way of avoiding a heavy sentence.

We know little about his shop but it could certainly have been an outlet for contraband. He gave his occupation as 'Shopkeeper' again at the marriage of his son Thomas in 1840 but the 1841 Census records him as an Agricultural Labourer. When he died in January 1845, coming out of his bedroom and falling down the stairs, the local newspaper described him as a Shopkeeper. His widow Jane continued to live at 'The Ramblers' until her death in 1863.

The younger Thomas was also listed in the 1841 Census as an Agricultural Labourer, living with his wife in Sea Lane. But Kelly's 1845 Street Directory shows him as the Receiver (sub-postmaster). This might, possibly, have referred to his father but with a conviction for smuggling that seems unlikely. In the 1851 census Thomas, now aged 33, is described as a Coachman, probably for Edwin Henty because Henty had him appointed as Constable for Ferring - an office with occasional duties rather than an occupation. In 1855 the West Sussex Gazette reported that he served a summons on some gypsies for cutting wood to make rakes and clothes pegs. But he is listed in the Post Office Directory for 1851 as a Shopkeeper; presumably he and his wife ran the shop and the post office between them an

By the 1861 census Thomas the younger and his family (now eight children) have moved into The Ramblers with Jane (now 83). After her death Thomas took over the copyhold. In the 1861 census Thomas is finally described as a Grocer. In the 1871 census he and his wife Hannah have four children living with them. In the 1881 census Thomas is 63, described as a Labourer, and his wife 'a Grocer's shopkeeper'. Sons Frederick 29 and John 20, both labourers, are living with them. Thomas died in 1888.

The ownership of The Ramblers passed to his eldest son, yet another Thomas, but in 1891 the house was occupied by his sister Jane, married to John Saunders, and their brother Frederick.

His brother John was 30, an Agricultural Labourer married to Charlotte 29; with five young children, living at 2 Manor Cottages.

In 1901 the Saunders are still in the Ramblers and John is now a Farm Carter, 40; Charlotte 39; John 15, House boy; Arthur 13, Farm boy; Winifred and Margaret (twins) 8; Robert 4, and Percy 1. Their address at the census is Sea Lane Cottages - probably the old cottages opposite East Ferring Farm House (later rebuilt as 'Homestead Cottages'). The sons all served in World War I and John was killed in the Second Battle of Ypres in May in 1915.

Absentee Landlords

The Richardsons

The Richardson family have already been mentioned as landowners in East Ferring. They did not live in the parish in the 19th Century, although several of them are buried there. **William Westbrook Richardson II** (1788-1871) inherited the Ferring, Goring and Findon estate on the death of his cousin's widow Mary, in 1828. He lived in Findon Manor House, but was buried in Ferring (recorded as 'of Brighton, late Findon'). His grave is the large altar tomb just outside the church door. The tomb is also dedicated to his youngest brother, who had died two years earlier. The 25 acres at North Down were sold in 1817. William did not marry and his property seems to have passed to his mother's family, the Margessons. They presumably sold the Ferring land because the family's last 69 acres in Ferring (the old Manor Farm) as well as North Down ended up, along with most of the rest of East Ferring, in the possession of the Lyon family.

The Lyons

The Lyon family also had little to do with Ferring, apart from the acres they owned. **David Lyon (**1796 – 1872) was a rich merchant, owning 13 estates in the West Indies. He bought most of Goring from the Richardson family in 1835 and part of East Ferring from the estate of John Cortis in 1838, including East Ferring House. The property in Goring and Ferring was left to his brother **Major William Lyon**. The Major lived at Goring Hall and died there in 1892. The estate was left to his son **William F Lyon**, who died in 1925. Neither of these had any contact with Ferring apart from collecting their rents. It might be added that there is no evidence at all of the late Queen Mother's connection with this family, for all that her single name was Elizabeth Bowes-Lyon.

Sea Lane: Nineteenth Century Farm workers' cottages, replaced by Homestead Cottages early 1930s

Sea Lane: The 'Ilex' carriage drive to Goring Hall. West Lodge behind the left-hand gate.

CHAPTER 8: A FERRING CHRONICLE

The previous chapters have dealt with the century by themes – land ownership, the village economy, social life and other topics. In this chapter we record some incidents and events decade by decade, which gives a complementary view to life in Ferring in those 100 years.

THE FIRST DECADE

Census

The first-ever Census was taken on 10 March 1801. There was no record made of the parishes' households, or of individuals' names, ages, marital status, occupation or place of birth; only a total figure of males and females but it did record land use and crops, as discussed in Chapter 2. Ferring's population was counted as 238, made up of 123 males and 115 females. That figure reflected the employment capacity of the farms and the trades that served them and would have hardly changed from the figure for 100 years earlier. It barely grew over the following 100 years (only 253 at the 1901 Census).

Civil Defence

The Census would have been a one-day wonder for the population of Ferring; far more important in 1801 was the threat of invasion – by Napoleon's army across the Channel. In anticipation of this, a much more detailed inventory was made of Ferring's resources – human, material and logistical; of what it could offer in defence, what food it could provide for itself and locally based regiments, and how if necessary, it could be evacuated. This 'muster' was first made in 1801 and updated in 1803.

There were of course regiments of the 'regular' army in the south coast counties (including at one point, 5,000 soldiers at Clapham Common, at the back of Highdown), and a Volunteer Corps, or Militia, but the Government was also prepared to use boys of 15 and men of 60 (seen as elderly in those days), and was prepared to evacuate the remaining population and commandeer supplies and work animals.

Ferring is shown as having 54 men and boys between the ages of 15 and 60, all capable of active service; 4 men above 60 capable of active service and 6 incapable, but all 10 of them capable of leaving the area without assistance, together with 47 women and girls over 7 years of age; 22 women incapable (including breast-feeding mothers); 15 boys under 7 years, and 20 girls. No Ferring residents were in the Volunteer Corps, but at least there were no Aliens, and no Quakers, who would refuse to fight.

Indeed, all 54 men and boys of eligible age were prepared to 'do their bit'. Two could arm themselves with flintlocks, and nine with pikes. Another 16 were ready to serve as Pioneers (two equipped with felling axes, seven with pickaxes, three with spades and four with shovels). In addition, 27 were prepared to round up the livestock - nine to act as drivers of cattle, nine as drivers of sheep and nine as drivers of teams (probably of horses, for pulling waggons).

Of course, the invasion never came to pass. Napoleon did not attempt it in 1801 and settled his differences with Britain in the Peace of Amiens in 1802. When Britain came back into the war in 1804, Napoleon trained another army to invade but lost all opportunity of doing so when his navy was defeated at Trafalgar, and in any case by 1805 he was committed to fighting in central Europe, and later, in Russia.

Melancholy Accident

An incident reported in the Kentish Chronicle gives a flavour of what life was like in Ferring in this first decade of the century. On Sunday 5 March 1809 Francis Cunningham, aged 47, a shoemaker in Ferring, had been out collecting shoes for repair and having finished earlier than usual, said the newspaper report, had his dinner and set off with a friend, George Haines (also a Ferring resident), to a pub in Durrington, where they 'partook of some beer'. They had an argument about the best way home and Cunningham decided to go his own way. He went by a footpath through the fields, and along the bank of a stream, on a very dark night, when he stumbled into a drain and rolled into the ditch which had four feet of water in it.

He was heard calling out for help from 7pm till 2am but the villagers thought it was just a noisy group from the pub. He must have been desperately walking up and down the stream trying to find a way of climbing out, and evidently did so because his body was found next morning on the bank, well clear of the stream, but he was 'quite dead'. The inquest decided that he had 'Died through the inclemency of the weather'. Cunningham lived and worked at Rose Cottage (the house is still there, at the north-east corner of the modern Village Green), His son George took over the house and the shoemaking: he is listed in that occupation in the 1841 Census.

St Andrew's Church in 1804

The painting below is by Henry Petrie, The Dictionary of National Biography says. 'He was a faithful topographical artist, and before 1810 carried out a large number of sketches of historic buildings in southern England and northern France. Between about 1800 and 1809 he also painted several hundred watercolours, mostly of churches and castles in Kent, Sussex, Surrey, and Bedfordshire. Between about 1800 and 1809 he also painted several hundred watercolours, mostly of churches and castles in Kent, Sussex, Surrey, and Bedfordshire'. Note the partial view of the old Ferring Grange in the right background, and one of its barns in the left.

THE NEXT TEN YEARS

Census

The 1811 Census was carried out on the same basis as in 1801. The population had barely increased (to 243) but in the following ten years it increased by 17 per cent (to 285). There was no increase in the birth rate, or in the number of households (the labour force required on the farms did not change). However, the parish registers show that there were only 41 deaths in that decade compared with 87 in the previous decade, while the number of births was slightly lower, indicating a substantial improvement in health and life expectancy between 1811 and 1821.

The 1813 Map

The first Ordnance Survey maps of England, at one inch to the mile (1:63,360), were published in the first two decades of the Century: Kent and Essex in 1801, but Sussex not until 1813. The map below shows little detail but it is clear that 'West Ferring' was the major settlement, along Ferring Street; 'East Ferring' was a group of houses along Sea Lane, 'Hangleton' referred to the houses north of the Rife, on both sides of Littlehampton Road. The group of houses at the north end of Ferring Lane is not named here but 'Franklands (or Franklins) Green' appeared on later maps. Highdown is clearly shown, with the windmill very prominent.

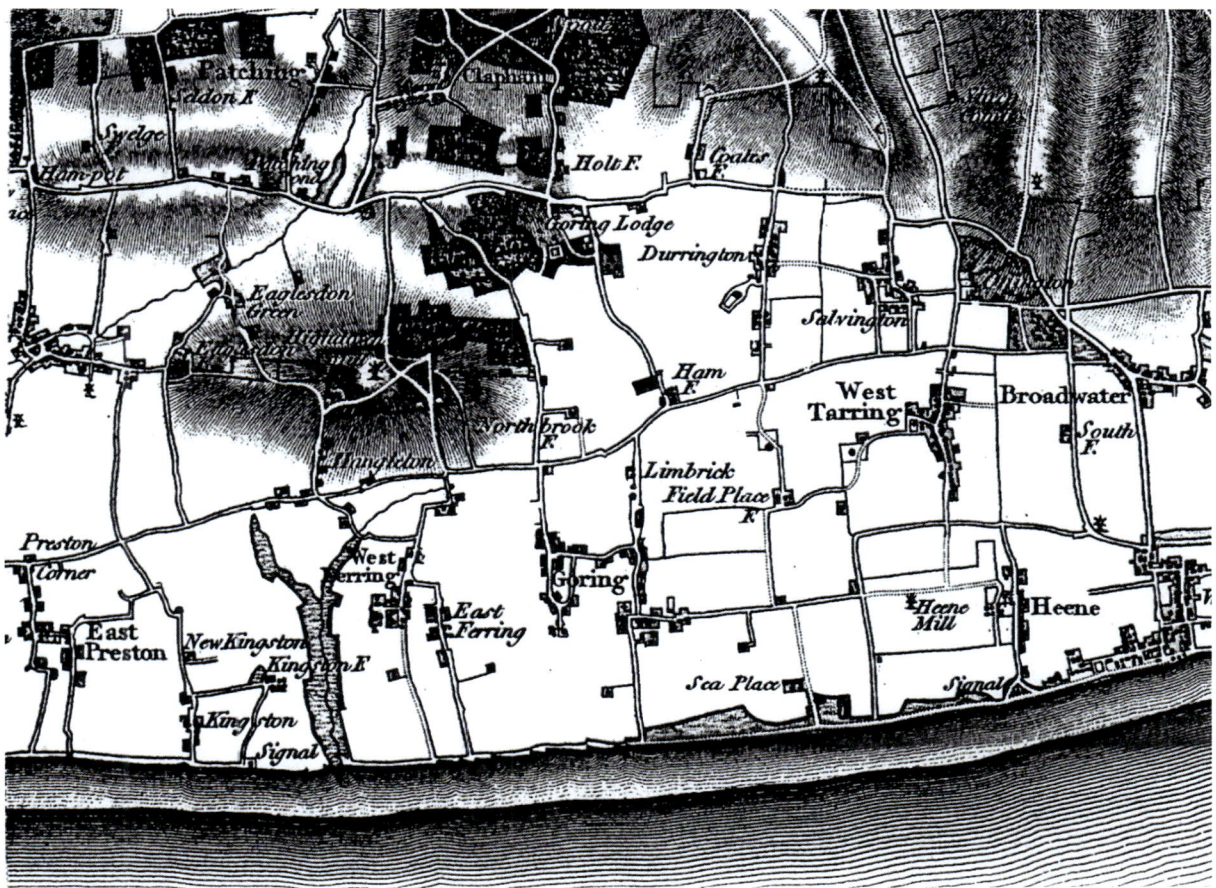

Section of the Sussex sheet of the Ordnance Survey map, first edition 1812

It is interesting to note the road that continues south from Ferring Street, passing the old Manor House and continuing to the beach. This was also shown on the 1621 plan of the manor estate but was probably closed up when Edwin Henty remodelled the 'Lower Farm' and separated his 'gentleman's residence' from it in the 1830s. The road was not shown on the 1837 map that was the basis of the Tithe Rent Charge Agreement of 1840, but the line of it could still be seen in the field boundaries in later maps - and in Jersey Road in the 1932 map. The small rectangles shown on the west side of this road and the east side of Sea Lane appear to be the two ponds later known as 'Little Paddocks pond' and 'Palmer's pond' (right on the Goring boundary). Note also, the marshy meadows along the Rife, frequently flooded before the embankments were built up in the 20th Century.

The Henty Smuggling Case

The trials of George Henty in 1818 for smuggling, and of the principal witnesses for perjury later that year, throw some light not only on the prevalence of that crime in this decade but also on the employment and social relations of the time.

George Henty was charged with organising the unloading and 'receiving into his custody' a large quantity of smuggled spirits. The prosecution, for the Excise Department alleged that in the early hours of 4 April 1817 a lugger (a small ship) landed 300 'ankers' (casks) of Geneva (gin) at the bottom of Sea Lane. The prosecution said the cargo taken to a barn in Henty's farmyard (at this time this was immediately outside the Manor House (Ferring Grange)) and hidden there, and that George Henty had organised the operation. Henty denied this completely.

The prosecution said a large number of people had been employed to carry the casks to the barn, which the defendant locked. He then put the key in his pocket and went away. Witnesses were called, who supported this statement: William Souter, a farm worker from Kingston (an ex-soldier wounded at Vittoria) said that early on 4 April 1817 he was present when over 300 tubs ('ankers') were landed at Ferring Lane End. It was between 5 and 6 am. There were several people there that he knew – 'Charles Hill (a well-known smuggler), George Anderson, Mr West and a man called Winton'. Some 150 of these tubs were taken to Henty's barn, a very short distance from his house. George Anderson (one of Henty's employees) had already pleaded guilty in a linked case, and said he had accompanied his master that morning,

William Holles (a fisherman) and George Slater (road mender) also testified to the spirits being landed. Slater said Hill, Anderson, Winton, James Bennett, William Baker and others were there. All worked for Henty; Anderson was his groom, Hill was his carter. Spirits were taken to the barn (Henty was there, they said) and concealed. In cross-examination Sowter said he could see Mr Henty in court. It was about 5.30 when the lugger came in. There were about 30 men there. He was unsure how long it took to unload and take away the tubs. He (reluctantly) admitted that he had been a witness in two other trials and had been admonished by the Judge. Slater, cross-examined, said it was between 6 and 7am when they had done. He saw Mr Henty later in the day, too

Henty's Counsel said there were only three witnesses and 'a more villainous description of witnesses never entered into a conspiracy together'. He called other witness to prove an alibi.

His Counsel said the admissions of the defendants 'in the last case '(presumably before the same court earlier that day) indicated that there had been a major smuggling offence on 4 April but the involvement of Mr Henty was concocted by corrupted witnesses. Sowter had prevaricated about his previous history as a witness, and mis-identified George Henty in court. Holles had seen smuggling but had not referred to Henty. Slater said he had seen Henty as late as 7 am, but Henty had an alibi from after 6 am.

James Henty then testified that he and his father left their house at Ferring between 5 and 6 am, in the gig, to catch the Worthing to London coach at Offington. The coach came at 8 am – he had been with his father all the time since 5.30 am. Cross-examined, he said his father had been out of his sight for 5 or 10 minutes between getting up and going off in the gig. Anderson had come with them to Offington on horseback and rode back with the gig. The coach driver corroborated the story, as did Henty's son in law, a vicar, who met them in London.

Respectable citizens were produced to discredit Sowter's and Slater's trustworthiness.

The Judge, summing up, referred to Anderson as having pleaded guilty (presumably in the 'previous case') and having apparently accompanied Henty 'on the very morning the smuggling transaction took place, and manifestly after its completion'. He also commented on the fact that Henty had not produced any of his servants as witnesses.

Henty was convicted, with 'damages' of £1,000, plus three times the duty payable, in spite of his very good alibi and the dubious character of the main witnesses. He pressed for Sowter and Slater to be prosecuted for perjury.

The Perjury trial
In this trial, reported in the Times of 12 December 1818, the Prosecution Counsel said the lugger was supposed to have landed the cargo between 6 and 8 am – but this was low tide and it would have needed boats and a lot of time to unload such a cargo. In any event, Henty had an alibi, Sowter was not there either, and there was no such smuggling transaction as described.

Phineas Belchamber, Henty's bailiff, said he had seen Henty and his son on their way to Offington at 5.30 am that morning. Belchamber had been in all the barns that morning and had seen no tubs. He kept the keys, not Mr Henty. Thomas Mills, Henty's foreman at another of his farms, at Offiington, said he saw Edwin Henty arrive there at about 6.15 am. Charles Hill was working in the farmyard that morning and said he saw no tubs in the barn that morning (however, he admitted under cross examination that he had seen some there on the evening of that day, and had hidden them in a nearby hedge), John Winton, whom Souter had said was unloading the lugger that morning, said he was not there. He admitted that he been involved in a smuggling operation that evening and that George Henty had no part in it.

Another witness, James Harmer a boatman in the Revenue service, said he had walked the beach from Ferring to Goring at sunrise and had seen no lugger. Finally, Souter's landlady, in Shoreham, testified that he was still in bed at 5am that day and had not got up until 7 am. Souter's Counsel then abandoned his defence and the jury quickly found him guilty.

The trial of Slater relied on the same evidence: the landlady testified that he too was at Shoreham at 7 am that morning. It was revealed that Slater had worked for Edwin Henty but had been discharged and subsequently denied Parish Relief 'through the intervention of Mr Henty, for which he had been heard to say he would have his revenge'. Slater was sentenced to transportation for seven years; Sowter was sentenced to two years in Horsham prison.

It is difficult to see why the Excise officers prosecuted such a flimsy case against a respected landowner. There had been smuggling at Ferring that day (seven of the smugglers were later convicted of it) and two of those who had been involved were willing to implicate Henty. The Excise officers were only too willing to believe them and thought they had landed a 'big fish', and it is possible that they made some kind of 'plea bargain' with the two who testified against.

Henty. Ferring villagers obviously did not believe his accusers because they subscribed to a trophy vase, now in Worthing Museum, commemorating his triumph.

The inscription reads, 'This Pedestal was presented to Mr Henty as a token of public respect for his spirited conduct towards suppressing the villanous informers supported by the Excise in the year 1818'.

THE EIGHTEEN-TWENTIES

Census

The 1821 Census showed 285 inhabitants, a substantial increase on the 1811 figure. It dropped back to 258 in 1831.

Highdown Mill

It was in this decade that Highdown Windmill closed down. The first windmill there had been erected around 1190 by Seffrid II, Bishop of Chichester. He recorded that had 'granted to Thomas de Ferring, for his service to the Church of Chichester and myself, the windmill at Ecclesdon Down which I made at my own costs, with two acres on the north next to the road that belongs to the mill, also the breadth of an acre all round outside the outer end of the beam by which the mill is turned round; and for all who wish to do suit to the mill or go there for any other business, a right of way to the mill from every part of the town'. The windmill blew down several times over the next 700 years but was always rebuilt as a 'post' mill, suspended from a huge centre post and turned round for the sails to catch the wind.

In the 18th Century it had belonged to the Richardson family and between 1750 and 1793 the tenant was John Olliver, the eccentric miller who, after the death of his wife, lived in a cottage up on Highdown, 200 yards away, just a few feet inside the Goring parish boundary. His nephews. George and Edward Olliver were working the mill with him towards the end of his life (he died at 84) and perhaps into the new century (it was shown on the 1813 Ordnance Survey map) but it may have been abandoned for a year or two before Edward Olliver advertised the mill gear for sale in 1827. The sale, as announced in the Sussex Advertiser, included not only the grindstones, gear wheels and sail-cloths of the mill but also several cows, two carthorses, various waggons. two ploughs, harrows, a threshing machine and other 'husbandry implements', – in effect a small farm, based on the 'Miller's Croft' and perhaps another property in north Ferring which John Olliver had bequeathed to his nephews.

A new mill had been erected a few hundred yards to the west, in Angmering, in 1826, and this no doubt served the wheat-producing farms of Ferring for the next few decades.

George Henty and his legacy

George Henty's father, William Henty, had bought the lease of the Bishop's demesne land from the Shelley family in 1786. William had been a very successful farmer and owned land in Littlehampton, Rustington and East Preston. He died in 1796 having left those estates to his younger son Thomas, and the Ferring estate to George, the elder son.

Thomas sold his inheritance and bought Church Farm in Tarring, thereafter going out to join his sons in Australia. George, 30 years old when he inherited, seems to have run the Ferring farm efficiently but he had other business interests, In 1808, with Thomas, he joined two other local men of property in founding the Margesson, Henty, Henty & Hopkins Bank, which by the time of his death in 1829 had branches in Worthing, Arundel and Steyning. In 1827 he bought a brewery in Chichester. The bank eventually grew to six branches and still survived under the Henty name until 1896, when it was taken over by the Capital and Counties Bank. The brewery (which also owned many public houses) continued under the family name for the next 130 years, having merged with the Constable Brewery in 1921.

The Bank was robbed in 1826. A £1,000 parcel of banknotes, which was being sent to Brighton by the Southampton to Brighton coach, was stolen. James Henty testified that on 16 August he had locked the parcel in the strongbox of the coach when it stopped at the innyard at Worthing but when the strongbox was unlocked at Brighton it was empty. Thomas Hollingshead was charged with the robbery but acquitted for lack of evidence. However, a letter, dated September, 23 1826, was posted to Mr James Henty, who had replaced Thomas as the other family director, and read as follows:-

" SIR, - the Party that Robbed the Coach of your Parcel is Richard Collard and the two Brothers Names Nightingales and Wm. Wellch and Richard Childs and Coachman will now him and the other Partys as well and you are sure to gett your money Off them if they are taken but you must Keep their Names as Private as Possible or Else they will gett out of Reach and be sure to keep there Names Private and ask Ellis if he dont now them but not show him this letter. I remain, -a Friend."

This implies that the coachman's name was Ellis, but at the trial the coachman testified as Thomas Holter. There are no reports of any of those named in the note being charged with the robbery.

George Henty had lived with his parents in Ferring and married Ann Penfold, daughter of the Vicar (and substantial landowner), in June 1790. Some scandal must have been created when a daughter was born in December of that year. He and Ann went on to have six more daughters and five sons. He left them all very well provided for. His will ran to 15 large pages. When he died in 1829 Robert and George inherited the brewery and Edwin inherited his stake in the bank, and the Ferring estate.

THE EIGHTEEN-THIRTIES

Census

The 1831 Census still did not list individuals or households but it did give aggregate figures in each Enumeration District for occupations or social status, Ferring had five farmers employing labourers, 44 agricultural labourers, nine craftsmen or retailers, one 'capitalist or professional' and four 'others'. The 'capitalist' was presumably Edwin Henty, as a banker, and among the 'others' would have been the Vicar, Henry Dixon. But this category cannot have included the servants – there were 28 of these in the 1841 Census.

The First Shop

Thomas Winton, was recorded as a Shopkeeper in the Parish Register entry for his son's christening in 1815, and again for the son's wedding in August 1840. He was born in Ferring, in 1774, and bought the house (now known as The Ramblers) backing onto the churchyard, in 1808. This was almost certainly where he had his shop. He may well have sold contraband there because he was one of those named in the 1818 smuggling case, and his grandson said in a 1941 newspaper interview that both his father and grandfather had been smugglers.

Tax and tithes

The Land Tax (at 25 per cent of the rental value of all but the smallest holdings) had been levied all through the 18th Century but local records only survive for the period between 1780 and 1832 (because they were evidence of the right to vote before the 1832 Reform Act changed the basis of the franchise). The 1832 schedule for Ferring showed that Edwin Henty was assessed at £373 a year rental value, two-thirds of the total for the parish. This includes the land he was about to inherit from his mother. The only other substantial landowners were John Bennett, John Cortis, and Hugh Ingram,

Tithes (nominally a tenth part of the annual yield of the land, due to the Church) go back to mediaeval times. In Ferring the Rector received the 'great' tithe – that on the cereal crops, and the Vicar received only the 'small tithes' on other crops and animal produce. The Rector was one of the Cathedral clergy (the Prebendary of Ferring) but successive post-holders leased out the 'Rectory Estate' (7 acres and the income from the great tithes) to laymen (at this time to Edwin Henty). By the 1830s, the payment of tithes 'in kind' was becoming too difficult to administer and an Act of 1836 set out the basis for a new national system of monetary payments based on the rental value.

The first step was a detailed survey and map of all the land ownership (and whether freehold), acreage, occupancy, use (arable, grass, orchard, wood) and assessable value. The map for Ferring was drawn up by Henry Salter, Surveyor, in 1837. It identified 209 parcels of land, including cottages and their gardens. Then came the schedules of ownership and occupation, and acreages. Last came the more difficult task of assigning and agreeing the amount of annual payment to be made for each parcel, either to the Vicar or to the (lay) Rector, in lieu of tithes. A report was made in 1838 but the 'apportionments' were not confirmed until February 1840.

The monetary values are of little interest now but the map and schedules give local historians a detailed record of who owned all this land, by what names it was known, who farmed it and whether it was for arable or grazing. The field names often hark back to earlier times – for example the Common Field, Sawpit Field, Gun Field, The Old Grattan, and Newfoundland.

The latter name is often found in documents of this period – not a direct reference to the Canadian province but rather a pun for newly cleared land.

Agricultural Labourers meet on Highdown

There was much unrest among farm workers in Britain in the 1830s. 1830 Sussex was one of the centres of the 'Swing' Riots and Edmund Bushby was hanged for setting fire to a hay rick in East Preston. Agricultural wages continued to fall and in February 1834 five farm workers from Tolpuddle in Dorset were arrested for trying to form a Trade Union. Next month they were sentenced to seven years transportation. On 6 November 1834 the London Standard published the following report of strike action in Goring.

The spirit of discontent among the rural population of this county has, we regret to find, already commenced in this neighbourhood. The price of wheat having declined to the ruinous sum of £9 and £10 per load, the wages have in consequence reduced, though not by any means in proportion to what flour can now be purchased at, and it is a fact that 10s a week at this time will buy more provisions than 12s would at the same time last year. On Monday last the farm labourers in the parish of Goring struck for higher wages, and obliged those who were unwilling to follow their example to leave their work, using threatening language to enforce arguments; in consequence the ploughs and teams were all deserted, and it appears as if the principle of the Trades Unions was about being established, for a very large assemblage of the labourers took place upon High Down Hill, a commanding eminence, overlooking the parishes of Goring, Ferring, Angmering, Tarring, &c.

At this moment affairs assumed an unpleasant aspect; the farmers and occupiers immediately waited on Captain Pechell, at Castle Goring; and decisive measures were taken to frustrate any of the attempts that were made during the disturbances in 1831 and 1832. Warrants were issued, and informations taken against those who had forced others to leave their master's service and his property in danger, and the land occupiers have agreed to discharge all those who voluntarily absconded and joined the mob, and to call in aid and assistance from the adjoining parishes. The labourers, after meeting early on Tuesday morning, soon after separated, and it is to be hoped that the usual quiet will be resumed, as it is clear that the display of their meeting on High Down Hill, to cause the other parishes to join, proved a signal failure. The Earl of Surrey's corps of yeomanry, as well as the mounted guard, were all ready for giving assistance at a moment's notice, which gives great security to all property in that part of the country.

THE EIGHTEEN-FORTIES

Demographics

The 1841 Census is the first really useful one for local historians, supplying individuals' names, approximate ages, occupations and whether born in Sussex or not. It did not, unfortunately, record the address of the household but the sequence followed by the enumerator helps to locate many of the premises.

There had been a 10 per cent increase in population since the 1831 Census. Only five of the 285 were recorded as born outside the county. The dominant occupation (usually shown for only the head of the household) was 'Agricultural Labourer', or simply 'Labourer' (35 cases). Others associated with farming were 'Farmer' (seven cases) and one 'Gardener' (i.e. smallholder). There were eight building tradesmen (three carpenters, two joiners, a sawyer, a stonemason and a bricklayer. Surprisingly, there were five shoemakers; less surprisingly, in a coastal village, one sailor. The rest were the two professionals (Banker and Vicar), two 'of independent means', and 28 servants. Eleven households included servants. William Marshall had six, Edwin Henty had five, the Vicar had four and Thomas Trussler had three. The rest were 'singles', usually listed in agricultural workers' households and sometimes helping a widower with young children, or simply lodging there while working at one of the big houses.

Thomas Winton is listed in the Census as an Agricultural Labourer, despite his occupation being entered as 'Shopkeeper' in the Parish Register of 1840. It may be that his shop was only a sideline and that the Enumerator's entry was more realistic but in January 1845 the Brighton Gazette reported that 'Mr Thomas Winton, of Ferring, shopkeeper, an elderly person, was coming from his bed-room in the morning, he fell down-stairs, and fractured his skull'.

The Railway

The biggest physical change in Ferring, in the 1840s or the whole of the Century, was undoubtedly the coming of the railway. The South Coast Railway had its origins in the 'industrial' railway built from Shoreham Docks to Brighton in 1840, as a means of transporting the materials to Brighton for the construction of the southern stretch of the London to Brighton line and the building of Brighton Station. This line was subsequently used for general freight and passengers.

Edwin Henty and others then formed a company to build a connection between Shoreham and Worthing and Chichester - the Brighton and Chichester Railway Company. The Shoreham to Worthing section was opened in 1840.

The route across West Sussex was surveyed in 1843. The land was purchased, and the track was laid down quite easily along the flat land. There were only two rivers to cross, the Adur at Shoreham and the Arun south of Arundel. In July 1845 the Brighton Gazette advertised invitations to tender for building numerous stations along the line – including one at Ferring but there must have been second thoughts about the viability of so many stations and several of them, including Ferring, were not built.

The route through Ferring, from 'The Butts' field on the Goring boundary, to Ferring Street and then just south of Langbury Lane out to 'The Nine Acres' on the Angmering boundary, was less than a mile long. A wide strip of land was bought from the various owners (including Henty himself) but the Company later sold back the land they did not need. In 1845 Edwin

Henty sold another piece of land, just north of the site of the level crossing and intended station, to his two brothers, who ran the Henty Brewery.

The Worthing to Chichester section opened in March 1846 and four months later the Brighton and Chichester Railway Company merged with others to become the London Brighton and South Coast Railway. That company did not build the hoped-for station but the site was in any event a good strategic location for an inn or public house, at the junction of the two main roads through the village. The Henty brothers bought the freehold in 1850 and the 'New Inn' was opened in 1851.

There were only a few trains a day in the early years but the closing of the level crossing gates even then caused some inconvenience and bad temper. Three years after the opening, Henty had the LBSCR Company taken to court for failing to operate the crossing properly. The *Brighton Gazette* reported the case as follows. Edwin Henty was going back to his house (Ferring Grange, just behind the church) on the night of 24 September 1849, and found the level crossing gates closed, and locked, against him (the barriers at that time were large pairs of wooden gates swung manually by the crossing keeper). He told Arundel Magistrates Court that he called out to the gatekeeper but there was no response. He then rang the bell, put there to attract the keeper's attention, and 'the man, after delaying him seven or eight minutes, opened the gate'.

Whether he muttered something under his breath we are not told but Henty, who by this time owned or leased half of Ferring, was not at all pleased. He reported the facts to the Parish 'Waywarden' (Thomas Trussler – one of his tenant farmers) and got him to take out a summons against the railway company for 'not having appointed a proper person to attend the opening and closing of the gates crossing the railway at Ferring'. When the case came up, the solicitor for the company asked, 'How long after you rang the bell, were you detained?' (Henty: 'Five minutes'). 'Had you rung the bell in the first instance that would have been the length of your detention?' (Henty: 'Probably so, but I ought not to have had the trouble to ring or call as the Company have no right to shut down and fasten the gates across a public highway').

The Chairman of the Bench said, 'They have not only a right to shut the gates but are compelled by the Act of Parliament to do so. In this instance the detention was longer than it ought to have been, and there must therefore be a fine: but the smallest sum will be sufficient to meet the case. Fined one shilling'.

THE EIGHTEEN-FIFTIES

Census

The Census of 1851 showed a modest increase on the 1841 population, from 285 to 312, although the latter figure included a travelling family who were just passing through – a hawker, his wife and eight children. The farms seemed to be doing well. There were 69 Agricultural Labourers (the youngest aged 8, the oldest 83), and five tenant farmers and 15 house servants. Few other occupations are listed for women but there is one 'Grocer and Baker', three Dressmakers, one School Mistress and 'Gate Keeper No.38', wife of a 'Plate Layer', presumably living at the railway cottage,

Gentry and Traders

The Post Office Directory for 1851 divides the noteworthy inhabitants into 'Gentry' and 'Traders'. The Gentry comprised Richard Bine esq., Henry Dixon (the Vicar), Dr Newton Hanson, Edwin Henty, and Mrs Simmonds. Richard Bine was living with his father, Francis, (described as a 'Fundholder' in the Census for that year), aged 42, with a brother and sister of similar age (all unmarried). Francis died in 1857 but these adult children were still in Ferring in the 1861 Census. Richard and his brother were both described as Fundholders. Richard's death was registered on Worthing in 1863. Dr Hanson lived in the Square House, Edwin Henty in the Grange, and Susannah Simmonds in what is now Holly Cottage, Church Lane. She was 85 and owned 20 acres in north Ferring.

The Traders were John Cortis, John Golds, Thomas Meetens, Thomas Trussler (all farmers); Henry Holding (Carpenter and Parish Clerk), Thomas Hide (boot maker), John Moore (beer retailer and bootmaker), Miss Eliza Moore, William Roots and Thomas Winton (all shopkeepers). John Moore was 48 in 1851, and although described as a Cordwainer in the 1851 Census, had been selling beer as a sideline since at least 1845. Now he was the first landlord of the New Inn, which was built a few years after the railway came through in 1846. He continued as landlord until at least 1855 but had reverted to shoemaking by 1858.

Eliza Moore was his niece, described as 'Grocer and Baker' in the 1851 Census. Her shop was probably in Landalls in Ferring Street. Thomas Hide's shoemaker's shop was probably in Smugglers Cottage at the far end of Ferring Street. He must have had a licence to sell beer (required since 1830) at this time but was convicted of selling it without a licence in 1870. William Roots was described as a Woodman in the 1851 Census and it is not clear what he was selling or where his shop was (probably his cottage in Franklins Green). Thomas Winton, aged 33, was listed as a Coachman (probably to the Hentys) but was also the postmaster, operating out of 'The Ramblers', the house and shop inherited from his father. Since letters had to be posted and collected from there this combination was no doubt profitable.

The Directory for 1855 shows little change: Edward Perronet Sells (a retired coal Merchant) is a new recruit to the Gentry, Mrs Bennett (widow of John Bennett) comes in as a farmer (John had 50 acres based on Hangleton Grange in the 1851 Census), Samuel Saunders has taken over the 'Lower Farm' and Home Farm House from John Golds, but William Roots and his shop have disappeared. Another source shows Thomas Winton as the Parish Constable in this year.

Cricket

The first mention of a Cricket Club in Ferring is in an advertisement in the West Sussex Gazette of 12 May 1859:

'TO THE GENTLEMEN AND MEMBERS OF THE ANGMERING, RUSTINGTON, FERRING AND KINGSTON CRICKETING CLUBS.
R Heath, of Angmering, begs to inform the gentlemen and members of these clubs, that he has a new and good variety of COLOURED and WHITE flannels, for Trowsers. Also the newest and best colored SHIRTING FLANNELS, for the season, to which he solicits an early inspection, Also Lillywhite's Registered CRICKETING BELTS'

This very early mention of a Ferring 'Club' is surprising: the mention of a Kingston Club even more so, given their small populations; but Mr Heath presumably knew his market.

Henty the Banker

Henty & Co made a return under the Companies Act in 1859 showing the two directors as Edwin Henty, Ferring. gentleman, and George Henty, Chichester, gentleman. Business carried out at Arundel, Horsham, Steyning, Worthing. *from Brighton Gazette 24 February 1859*

The Great Pork Robbery

The West Sussex Gazette reported a strange case in August 1854. James Belchamber was a labourer on John Bennett's farm in Langbury Lane, probably living in Hangleton Cottages:

'Some person or persons entered the house of Mr Belchamber. at Ferring, and stole therefrom some pork, tobacco, money &c, on Sunday 24th. From enquiries made by Superintendents Ratigan and Norman, they have reason to suspect two men. One about 50 years of age, with a blue Gurnsey shirt and blue coarse trowsers, and with a leather belt around the waist, and with large features and dirty appearance. The other about 24 years of age, dressed in a brown shooting jacket, dark trowsers and black hat. They slept at a lodging-house at Worthing on Sunday, where they were seen to have about 1½ lbs of pork. wrapped in a newspaper. and a quantity of tobacco which they liberally gave away. They paid for what they had in copper, and left at about 8 o'clock the morning after the robbery. They passed through Findon toll-gate about three hours afterwards

'No doubt exists but they committed the robbery, as Mrs Belchamber saw a man answering the description of the oldest run from the back of the house on her return, but did not suspect anything wrong until she found the parlour in disorder, the front door unlocked, and a pane of glass broken in the parlour window. These men, unfortunately, have not been apprehended as Mr Belchamber neglected giving information until noon on the Monday, during which time the guilty parties had time to get out of reach of the district constables'.

THE EIGHTEEN-SIXTIES

The 1861 Census showed 253 inhabitants, almost 20 per cent less than in 1851 but reverting to the long-term average for the Century.

First photographs

Three photographs taken at Ferring in the 1860s have survived. They are probably taken by the same person and have an inscription, 'At Ferring' and the dates 1863 and 1864.

The first photograph was almost certainly taken at the Vicarage, and the couple in the picture, looking very much at home, are almost certainly the Rev. Henry Dixon and Mrs Anne Dixon (she died in March 1864). The next is more puzzling: it appears to be taken at the rear of the house we now call Greystoke Manor – then named St Maurs. This was owned at that time by Robert Hughes but he does not figure in the 1861 Census or the 1867 Street Directory. The house was probably occupied at that time, and until his death in 1873, by Edward Sells, a 'retired Coal Merchant' from Surrey. The third is even more puzzling: some of the faces resemble those in the second photograph but the location does not seem to correspond to any of the houses we know today, and no houses of that size seem to have been demolished between then and now.

Henty's acquisitions

Edwin Henty had been acquiring copyhold land since he succeeded his father as the lessee of the Bishop's estate in 1829. In 1830 he bought Franklands ('Manor') and the row of cottages to the south. On the death of his mother in 1832, he inherited the Penfold lands, and continued to acquire property in the 1840s and 1850s, by purchase. He bought Evergreen, May Tree and what was known later as Smugglers Cottage in 1863 and 'The Old Cottage' at the south end of Ferring Street, Holly Lodge and 9 acres in 865, then Highdown Hill Cottage with another 9 acres in 1866.

He had also bought the freehold of his various properties when this became possible under mid-Century changes in land law. This included the freehold of Ferring Grange (up to that point leasehold in 1864 and we must assume that its mid-Victorian appearance in the earliest photographs (40 years later) dates from that time, or even the 1870s. The diary of his niece, Agnes, a frequent visitor between 1864 and 1869, records much domestic and local detail but does not mention any rebuilding of the old house, and a local guidebook of 1912, 'The Sussex Coast' by Ian Hannah refers to 'Ferring Grange, a large modern house' (p.30). It seems, from its footprint in successive large-scale maps, that the house was modernised and extended and not entirely rebuilt.

THE EIGHTEEN-SEVENTIES

The Census
The 1871 Census figure was 267, a 5 per cent increase in population over 1861 and a total not exceeded until 1931.

The School
As noted in Chapter 4, the 'National' school was opened in January 1873, in Ferring Street just north of the Vicarage, on the south-eastern edge of the Vicar's Glebe land. The first teacher, Charlotte McIlwain, wrote in the School Log, 'I commenced duties at this, my first school,. Twenty-five children were admitted. On examining them, I found that, owing to there never having been a proper School in the village, they were very backward in writing and arithmetic; and also wholly undisciplined'. Charlotte did not stay long: she was followed by Caroline Russell in 1875, Eliza Dredge in 1876, and Ellen Laker in 1880. Ellen made her home in the village and continued as headmistress until 1919, when she was 60.

Alterations to Vicarage 1871
Henry Dixon died in office, in the Vicarage in November 1870. He was 72, and his wife had died in 1864. There were no children and Dixon had probably not changed the house much in the 35 years he had lived there. . His successor, the Rev, Gregory Pennethorne, was a young man of 34, and the 1871 Census shows him living with his wife, young son, a nephew, a niece, a governess and a pupil of 17. It is not surprising that he immediately drew up plans for alterations to the old building; enlarging and modernising it. This is the building we see today.

Henty wedding
In May 1872, Edwin Henty's youngest daughter, Maria, married Mr Stephen Fuller at St Andrew's Church. The West Sussex Journal reported, gushingly, 'The marriage was made the occasion of much rejoicing in the village of Ferring. The bride's kindness to the poor of the district, and the interest she has always taken in the Sunday school, no doubt tended to increase the warmth of the public manifestations. The attempts at floral decorations, in honour of the event were quite remarkable. Such a display of bunting we should think was never before displayed in the village; and that the resources of the good folk were sorely tried was evident from the exhibition in one roadside garden of a gay coloured shawl suspended on high and topped with a modest bunch of wallflowers. Across the road, near the entrance to Mr Henty's residence – the Grange - was erected a triumphal arch, somewhat primitive indeed in its execution and design but design and execution but nonetheless effective in its general result and in the cordiality of the sentiment to which it gave expression'.

Henty and Lyon exchange land
In 1878 Edwin Henty (who owned much of West Ferring) and William Lyon (who owned much of East Ferring) came to an agreement to exchange various fields to make it easier to manage them. Some 60 acres were exchanged in each direction, so that Henty then owned most of West Ferring and Lyon most of East Ferring. This also involved the exchange of various cottages – Whittingtons (later Calgary Cottage) on the east side of Sea Lane going to Lyon and 'Homestead Cottages' and some associated farm buildings, on the west side of the lane coming to Henty.

The Village in 1876

Composite map from 1876 Ordnance Survey sheets

The Ordnance Survey 25 inches to the mile map shows little change from the 1813 map - only more detail. There are two distinct settlements – West Ferring around Church Lane and Ferring Street, and East Ferring around the old East Ferring Manor Farm on Sea Lane.

.THE EIGHTEEN-EIGHTIES

Edwin Henty seemed to dominate the history of this decade. He was a prominent churchman as well as a landlord, and banker. He paid for a substantial renovation of St Andrew's in 1887, having already paid for repairs and alterations in 1842 and 1876.[see church booklet] A Sussex newspaper reported its re-opening in April, noting that, 'This work, owing to the decay of the walls, assumed larger proportions than at first anticipated', and cost Henty £2,000 (£280,000 at 2022 values). It went on to say, 'In the course of restoration a disused passage was discovered which led by a winding staircase up to a no longer existing tower'. This is a considerable mystery – the church had been without a tower since the 16th Century, at least, and no other evidence has been found to support its existence.

Henty was very much involved in the Golden Jubilee celebrations in June 1887. The West Sussex Journal reported, 'The festivities took place in a meadow in front of the Grange, the residence of Mr E Henty. ... The funds (including a liberal donation from Mr Henty) that had been raised enabled the committee to instruct Mr Wilkinson of the Lamb Inn, Angmering, to provide a substantial dinner, in a tent, at which about 100 sat down.' After the dinner Mr Henty proposed a toast to 'The Queen of England and Empress of India, who he said, had ever shown sympathy with the cares and troubles of her people', followed by a speech on the blessings of her reign and the unity of the Empire. . After many other toasts 'the company joined in the sports provided in the field through Mr Henty's liberality. The women and children were regaled with tea in the tent at five o'clock, about 200 sitting down'.

There was also a bonfire prepared on Highdown, one of 50 at highpoints all over Sussex, each bonfire at least 35 feet high, to be lit at 10 pm, on a signal given by rockets from Ditchling Beacon.

Edwin Henty died on 31 January 1890, a few weeks short of his 85th birthday. He owned two-thirds of Ferring and was the senior partner in the family bank. The Sussex Advertiser commented, in reporting the death, 'Speculation as to his wealth would of course be out of place here; but it may be noted that one of the former partners of the same firm, Mr George Henty of Chichester died some time since leaving a personality of close on £400,000'. Edwin Henty did not leave quite so much in money (£144,000) but passed all his considerable property in Ferring to his wife Laura and his son Edwin junior, and his stake in the family banking business to Edwin and his other son, Arthur.

He had been a local magistrate since 1842 and Chairman of the Worthing Bench since 1868.

Edwin Henty jnr in the 1890s   by permission of Worthing Museum and Art Gallery

THE EIGHTEEN-NINETIES

Starvation

In August 1891, William Cortis the tenant of East Ferring Farm, was going home for his dinner when he spotted a shabbily dressed man' lying between his barn and a straw stack', unconscious. He felt his hand, which was quite cold, but he was seemed to still have some life left in him. He sent for the Overseer of the Parish and had the man removed to the Union Workhouse. The Overseertold the inquest that the man, apparently aged about 50, could not speak, and was a stranger in the district. The Medical Officer to the Union said he ordered the man to be put to be and given some nourishment but he was found dead later that evening.

When he carried out the post-mortem the doctor found the body 'very much emaciated. The body was very bloodless and the heart contracted. Death was due to want of food and exposure to the cold. It was a case of chronic starvation'. A Mrs Hills of Kingston said the man had come to her door two days earlier asking for water and she had seen him afterwards lying in some straw. She gave him some milk later (traces of which were found in his stomach) 'He said he had some work at Preston' and walked off.

The Coroner thought there was nothing suspicious about the death of the dececeased and the inquest jury returned a verdict of' death by chronic starvation and exposure to cold, accelerated by the bad state of the deceased's lungs'. The matter-of-fact way this death was reported in the Chichester Observer and West Sussex Recorder is rather shocking: why should anyone starve to death in the richest country in the world, how could exposure to the cold, in August, contribute to his death and why, if he was on his way to Preston, was he found dying in East Ferring?

The Hentys

Laura Henty continued to live at the Grange until her death in late 1897. Her son, Edwin Henty junior, had been living in Ifield, near Crawley, since his marriage in 1875, presumably overseeing the branch of the family bank there, but returned to Ferring by 1895, living at St Maurs (now Greystoke Manor) for the next five years.

Another Jubilee

Victoria's Diamond Jubilee in June 1897 was celebrated in Ferring in much the same way as the Golden Jubilee ten years earlier. Now it was Edwin Henty junior who stepped up to the plate. 'Residents of Ferring were indebted to[his] generosity for an excellent programme of festivities on Thursday [24 June]', enthused the Worthing Gazette. 'The Cricket Field was the scene of operations', decked out with bunting and other decorations. 'A commodious marquee was erected on the west side of the ground and within this structure about 80 of the male inhabitants of the parish sat down to a capital dinner'. The dinner was provided by the Hentys' domestic staff and at the close of the meal Mr Henty, like his father in 1887, 'submitted the toast of "The Queen", remarking on the progress that had been made in the 60 years of Her Majesty's reign. The National Anthem was sung and three hearty cheers were given'. There was a cricket match and the Goring Brass Band played. An abundant tea was provided for 140 women and children, Jubilee mugs were presented to the children and races were run for prizes.

A telegram was send to the Home Office conveying the respect and congratulations from the village of Ferring, assembled in honour of the Diamond Jubilee'.

That evening, once again, a large bonfire was lit on the top of Highdown, one of 83 on Sussex high spots. Rudyard Kipling, living in Burwash, no doubt saw similar bonfires in East Sussex and in his poem *Recessional* marking the Jubilee (and the end of a remarkable century) wrote,

'Far called, our navies melt away:
On dune and headland sinks the fire:
Lo, all our pomp of yesterday
Is one with Nineveh and Tyre!
Judge of the Nations, spare us yet,
Lest we forget – lest we forget.'

On 7 July 1897 the Worthing Gazette reported that a new Lychgate had been constructed for the entrance to St Andrew's churchyard' noting that, 'The cost of £35 was met by voluntary contributions from the parishioners and others'.

This contemporary photograph from the West Sussex Record Office shows the view from the churchyard. To the left can be seen the tiled roof of The Ramblers, and the thatched roof of Church Cottage on the other side of Church Lane. To the right is one of the pair of cottages owned by Edwin Henty and demolished by him in 1906 to provide an extension to the graveyard.

Excavations on Highdown
In 1892 Edwin Henty employed some workmen to plant a copse at the top of Highdown, perhaps in imitation of what Charles Goring had done at Chanctonbury Ring in 1760. As they dug the holes for the young trees they began to find a number of ancient graves, with many bones and many grave goods. Henty became aware of these discoveries and did his best to preserve them but the workmen were not his own employees and he guessed that many objects of value had been taken away and sold. David Garnett wrote a good account of what followed in the Ferring History Group's Newsletter in 2011:

'Henty was determined that this would not happen again when more trees were planted the following year. He approached Charles Hercules Read, who had been an assistant curator at the British Museum since 1880 and was also the Secretary of the Society of Antiquaries, to supervise a proper excavation. Read was familiar with the 1892 Highdown discoveries, one of which was already in the British Museum – an *angon*, a barbed iron javelin from east of the Rhine, 30 inches long. "In England," he wrote, "it is so rare as to be almost unknown". Other weapons, pottery, jewellery and tools were also found but no record was made of the finds or in which graves they were found.

The next Highdown excavation was in 1893, when Edwin Henty invited Charles Hercules Read back to Ferring to continue his work. Read is forced to admit that "the vigour of the men in digging (one of the graves) ended in disaster, for with a stroke of his spade he ruthlessly shattered a most charming glass bowl . . . This is the more to be regretted as it differs in ornament from any I have ever seen."

'Considering the speed of the excavations, it's a tribute to the diggers' skill that more relics were not destroyed. Henty and Read began work at Highdown on October 31, 1893, and the latter delivered his paper only thirty days later – after the excavation of thirty-two graves. At one point, he confesses to the haste of the work by admitting: "This grave had unfortunately to be hurried as the light was failing, and the positions (of the bones) in the grave are not certain." Read had to return to London in mid-November, and Edwin Henty supervised the rest of the work, cataloguing and measuring the finds ("with the most excellent of results," commented Read)'. Among the relics were brooches, glass and amber beads, silver rings, pottery cups and bowls, Roman coins used as ornaments, glass bowls and goblets, iron knives and swords and spear heads.

The next Highdown excavation was the following year, 1894, when Edwin Henty invited Charles Hercules Read back to Ferring to continue his work.

Edwin Henty kept many of the Highdown finds in his home, Ferring Grange. His widow donated the Highdown collection to Worthing Museum – where it is now on display.

1900 election
There was a general election in the Autumn of 1900 – in the middle of the Boer War - known to historians as the 'Khaki Election'. The war was going well at this point and Lord Salisbury expected the mood of patriotism to secure the continuation of his Ministry. So it did. Lord Edmund Talbot. grandson of the Duke of Norfolk, had been the Member of Parliament for South West Sussex since 1894, as a Conservative, and was easily returned in 1900. Two election meetings were held in Ferring (the first ever, noted the Parish Magazine) which, given that only male householders could vote, meant that the electorate could not have been more than 60. The MP had changed his surname from Fitzalan-Howard in order to benefit from the will of Bertram Talbot, 17th Earl of Shrewsbury

The End
The Century ended on Monday 31 December 1900. Queen Victoria was at Osborne House, aged 81 and entering her final illness, which ended 22 days later. There was only one resident of Ferring old enough to remember the reign of her predecessor, William IV. That was Dr William Kelley, aged 82, a cousin of Mrs Roberts at 'The Farm House', later known as 'Home Farm House'. It had been a remarkable reign and a remarkable Century but in reality little had changed in the farming village of Ferring.

Ferring in 1898

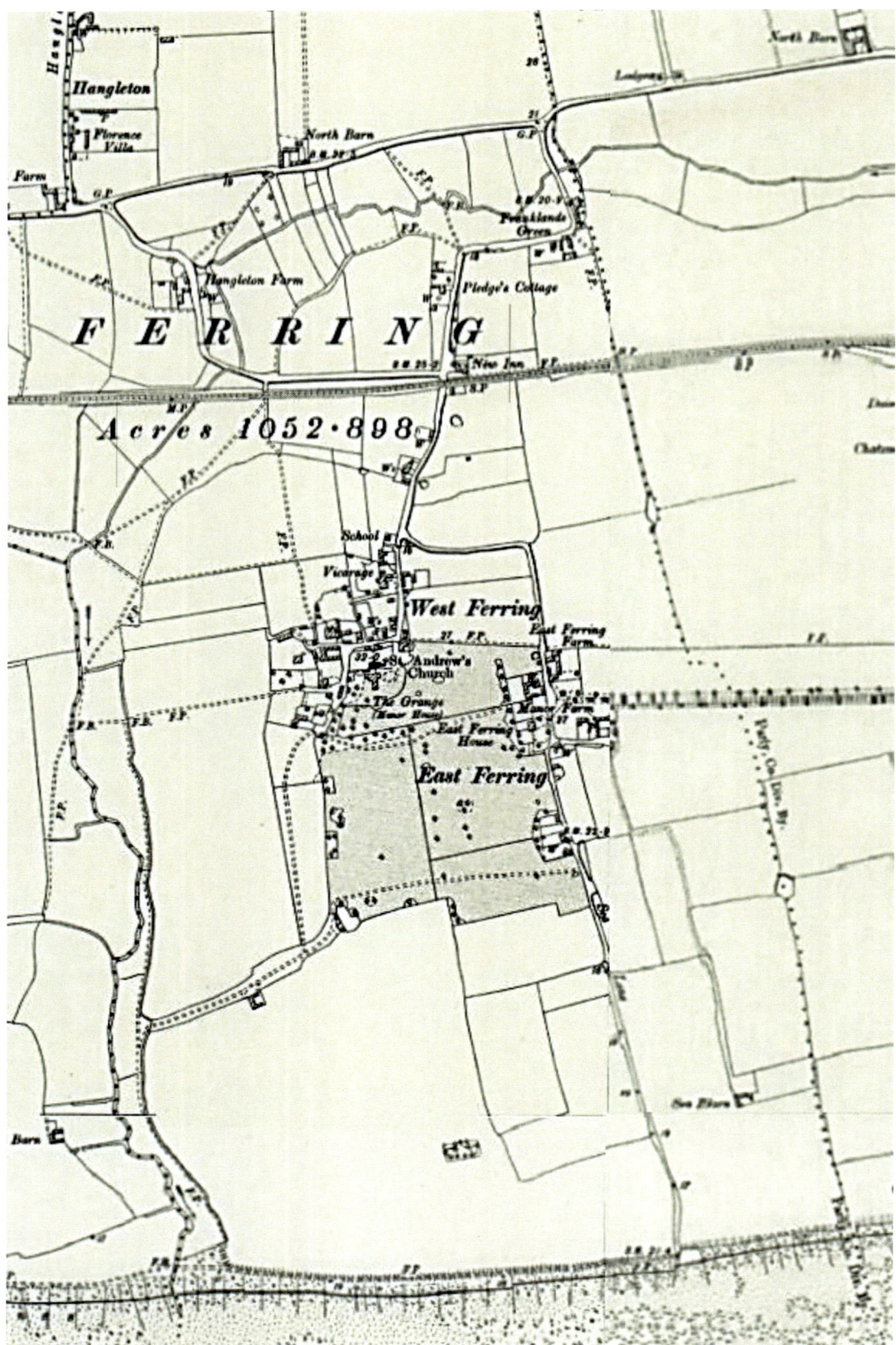

From the Ordnance Survey 6 inch map